# WESTCHESTER

## AN EARLY HISTORY OF WESTCHESTER & PLAYA VISTA CALIFORNIA

### (AND ENVIRONS)

DAVID J. DUKESHERER

CENTAL

Dedicated to preserving the memory of
Rancho's La Ballona & Aguaje Centinela

**DEDICATION OF MINES FIELD, 1928.** (Courtesy, LAPL).

**ON THE COVER: FANS AT LAX IN WESTCHESTER, WELCOME BACK THE LAST PLACE LOS ANGELES DODGERS, 1958.** (Complements, LAPL).

# WESTCHESTER

## AN EARLY HISTORY OF WESTCHESTER & PLAYA VISTA
### CALIFORNIA
### (AND ENVIRONS)

*FIRST EDITION*

D

Beach Of The King

The Early History of Playa Del Rey,
Westchester & Playa Vista, California

D J Dukesherer

**CENTAL Historical Group, Inc.**
Los Angeles, California USA
The Cental logo includes the Rancho La Ballona cattle brand.
www.rancholaballona.com

## Authors Note

*Wikipedia* describes Westchester as being located in the eastern part of the Del Rey Hills also known as the Westchester Bluffs. The Westchester community is separated from the Pacific Ocean by Playa del Rey on the west. Its northern border is defined by and includes the area now know as Playa Vista, as well as Culver City, and the unincorporated area of Ladera Heights. The Playa Vista community is located within the northern portion of Westchester. The city of Inglewood is to the east, and the city of El Segundo is to the south.

It is home to Los Angeles International Airport (LAX), Loyola Marymount University (LMU), and Otis College of Art and Design.

And my home.

It is difficult, if not in fact impossible to discuss Westchester and Playa Vista, without discussing Playa Del Rey; a subject I have written widely about in other titles. To save the reader as much repetition as possible, I have tried not to revisit much of those matters in this volume. Those books, are available for everyone, at the Los Angeles Public Library, through a gift from the author.

Likewise, it is difficult to tell this history without a brief understanding of the important roll the City of Inglewood played in the early development of the LAX Region and Westchester.

The following chapters cover the period from the beginning to the 1960's. This is the first of two volumes.

**D. J. Dukesherer, Los Angeles, CA, July 2010**

**SEPULVEDA BOULEARD EXTENSION, 1942.** Leaders are shown in a ribbon-cutting ceremony opening the newly-constructed extension of Sepulveda Boulevard from Slauson to Centinela. Behind them is a convoy of Army trucks and jeeps, which were the first vehicles to pass through. Left to right: A.N. George; Major Robert J. Kennedy; Capt. Robert H. Scott; a convoy lieutenant; S.V. Cortelyou; Blaine Walker; Pat French, cutting the ribbon; Amerigo Bozzani; Mayor G.E. Heaton of Culver City; Wm. Edwards; and G.N. Ainley. Photo dated: October 12, 1942. (Courtesy, Los Angeles Public Library).

With Love, to my *Ahijada's* (Goddaughters);
Cara Dukesherer-Harris,  Jennifer  Dukesherer, &
Margaret  Jay;
from your Uncle David.

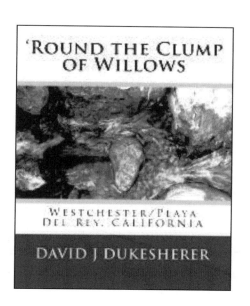

# CONTENTS

# ACKNOWLEDGEMENTS

This volume combines information from my personal writing, photos and vintage postcards, and from many other resources. Much of the information has been drawn from my monthly newspaper column, contained in *the Westchester Hometown News*, Los Angeles, CA, Robin Zacha, Publisher, in issues published between 2002 and 2008, and the *Westchester Hometown News*, 2009/2010, Stephanie Davis, Publisher.

I would like to thank the following institutions and their special collections which I am very grateful for; The Los Angeles Public Library (LAPL), the Santa Monica Public Library, the Loyola Marymount University Los Angeles Library, the Los Angeles Herald-Examiner Archives at the Los Angeles Public Library, the Fritz Burns Collection at the Loyola Marymount University- Charles Von der Ahe Library, the Pomona Public Library, the University of California at Los Angeles, the University of Southern California Library, the University of California Library, Berkeley, the University of Michigan, the LAX Coastal Area Chamber of Commerce, Patty Crocket, Google, Yahoo!, Doug Linnett/Playa Del Rey Photography, the Library of Congress: Prints and Photograph Division, Washington, D.C. , and the United States National Archives and Records Administration.

I would also like to thank the following for their special contributions and encouragement; Dace Taube of the USC Libraries, Susan Oppenheimer and Joe Atkinson of the Los Angeles Public Library, Playa Vista, CA Branch, Cynthia Becht of The LMU Charles Von der Ahe Library, Robin Zacha/Stephanie Davis, the Westchester Hometown News, A. B. "Brad" Fowler, Barbara Owens, Joe Callinan, P. M. Jay, Robert Jay, Maureen Jay, John Kielbasa, Peter Tompkins, John and Christine Wilson, and Doug Linnett.

**CENTINELA VALLEY, LATE 1800's.** (Courtesy, Wikipedia).

**STRAWBERRY FIELD, 1908**. This field is where the town of Playa Vista meets the Ballona Wetlands today. (Complements, Authors Collection).

# INTRODUCTION

*Well in to the 1940's, much of what we call Westchester, CA today, was sparsely populated farmland. What had developed along the great Pacific Ocean beaches beginning in the late 1800's, would eventually be known as Playa Del Rey, CA. Ancient bluffs; actually compressed sand dunes, meandering creeks, rivulets and one of the last great California wetlands separated the two areas. Together it was a paradise*

**from** *More from 'Round the Clump of Willows*

Although Westchester shares a place in history as part of the vast Spanish Land Grant called Rancho Sausal Redondo, the towns older cousins; Playa Del Rey, Venice, Culver City, Fox Hills, El Segundo and Inglewood, would be developed decades before. In fact, in 1928, when ground breaking began on the Jesuit Loyola University campus, about nineteen homes existed within the towns modern day borders. The town had remained a sleepy street- less farming town, with over 90% of the area dedicated to ranching and agriculture.

Some interest and notoriety was achieved , however, when in 1932, Westchester hosted the cross-county equestrian event for the 1932 Olympiad.

Along with the relocation of Loyola University; to Westchester; officially opened in 1929, two major issues would later drive the growth of the region.

First of all, the invention of the airplane, and later the commercial aviation industry, would create on land once set aside for dry farming, the mighty Los Angeles International Airport (LAX). Over 30% of all U.S. aircraft constructed for the great battles of World War II were made or designed in Westchester. Conveniently surrounding the airport, the Cold War fueled aerospace industry would be spawned, and the brightest and best scientists and engineers, would one day help put a man on the moon.

In 2009, LAX became the seventh largest airport in the world, with 56,520,843 passengers passing through its gates. This places LAX far ahead of other International Airports, including; Dallas/Fort Worth, John F. Kennedy International/New York, Frankfurt, Madrid, Hong Kong and Amsterdam.

Secondly, returning G.I.'s from World War Two flocked to Westchester, in search of a good climate, inexpensive housing, outstanding employment opportunities, and a new-clean community where they could raise a family.

The pace of construction; residential and the commercial infrastructure to support this mass exodus was mind boggling.

Within the towns borders; <u>roughly</u> Bellanca Avenue/Florence and La Cienega Boulevards to the east, Imperial Highway to the south( it is Playa Del Rey to El Porto along the seashore),  Centinela and/or Jefferson Boulevard to the north and Saran Drive to the west, development beginning in the 1940's  and continuing well into the 1960's, would create an area that today supports  39,315 souls.

Although the census  of 1910 did not enumerate Westchester area residents,  and the impoverished classes were generally not on the grid, it is estimated that no more than 60  full-time residents inhabited the area we today call Westchester.

Throughout history,  Westchester was called many things. During the California Rancho period, it was known as Rancho Centinela or *Guacho*, and later many referred to it as Playa Del Rey; sometimes Inglewood, Freeman, or Florence.  When Playa Del Rey, (Beach of the King),  was briefly annexed by Venice, the area shared this name too. And from 1929 until the 1940's, many folks simply called it, "Loyola."

The first seventy years has been a period marked by rapid growth and development, and to predict an end to this cycle is murky at best, with coalitions; developers and industry, creeping in and around like the fog that regularly blankets the region.

In 2001, a large chunk of Westchester, about 1100 acres; substantially the former world headquarters for the Hughes Aircraft Company, would be renamed; Playa Vista, California.

LAX continues to expand into the former residential and commercial area of the town, and with that growth a vibrant economic engine helps to sustain the many hotels, businesses, and tourist trade.

Writing a book can be at times an exigent task; and writing a book about a place that existed, but existed nameless, is very difficult. Until Fritz Burns acquired a former hog farm in the late 1930's, and began to develop the newly named town of Westchester around Manchester and Sepulveda Boulevard's, Westchester existed only as a no-mans land between Inglewood and Playa Del Rey. As I said, the area was almost completely dedicated to ; farming, the airport, and Loyola University.

Records of the farmers who inhabited this region between the late 1800's and early 1940's are almost nonexistent. There are signatures on deeds-of-trust and all that sort of thing, but a signature is worthless unless you can match a face to it when preparing a historical photo-documentary. They and their families have just fallen off the map. Photographs too, are far and few between, and when you look past the images of other places, you can see why; as far as the eye can see, Westchester was farmland. Few buildings even existed. Perhaps one day when I have some time, I can get a hold of someone's personal historical records, and reissue this book including those photos.

So needless to say, this book, and probably any volume on the subject of Westchester, California, is going to have quite a bit of information about the college and the airport. These two institutions, and perhaps the towns proximity to the wonderful mild sea-side weather, had more to do with the early memory of the area than anything else.

With the arrival of Hughes Aircraft in 1940, local war production and post war building boom, Westchester suddenly emerges from the pasture; and from a broader prospective, appears as though it was always there. It is almost unimaginable that anyplace could be developed as quickly as the town had been developed between 1940 and 1950.

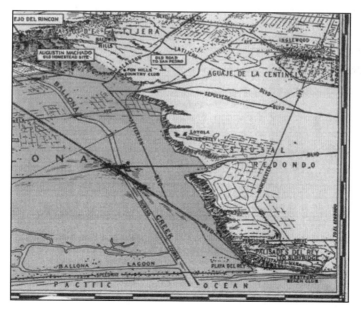

**76<sup>TH</sup> STREET AND SEPULVEDA BOULEVARD, LOOKING WEST TO 77<sup>TH</sup> STREET, 1948.** (Complements, Author).

# aut viam inveniam aut faciam

# *One*
## NATIVE AMERICAN ERA, EXPLORATION, COLONIZATION & THE MISSION ERA

Westchester, centered in Los Angeles County at 34 degrees latitude, (same latitude as Hiroshima, Japan), and 118 degrees longitude, and has an average elevation of 112.47 feet above sea level.

The history of the region begins with the migration of indigenous people traveling to the modern day Mohave, California area about 11,000 years ago. Eventually, around 200AD, they would move west to the Westchester Bluffs and Playa Del Rey area, and displace tribes of Chumash and *Hokan* speakers: perhaps Yana. They lived there undisturbed until the 1800's.

These people were known as the Tongva.

The Tongva , also referred to as the San Gabriel Band, are a Native American people who inhabited the area in Los Angeles County, California, before the arrival of Europeans. *Tongva* means "people of the earth" in the Tongva language, an Uto-Aztecan language.

The Tongva are also sometimes referred to as the Gabrielino-Tongva Tribe (Spanish: *Tribu de Gabrieleño-Tongva*) and the Fernandino-Tongva Tribe (Spanish: *Tribu de Fernandeño-Tongva*). Following the Spanish custom of naming local Mission Indian tribes after nearby missions, they were called the *Gabrieleño* in reference to Mission San Gabriel Arcángel.

Likewise, those in the San Fernando Valley and the nearby Tataviam people were known as *Fernandeño* after Mission San Fernando Rey de España.

Living in such a high growth area, many controversies have naturally arisen around land use issues relating to the Tongva. Conflicts between the Tongva and the rapidly expanding population of Los Angeles have often required resolution in the courts. Burial grounds have been inadvertently disturbed by developers. The tribe has complained about bones being broken by archeologists studying a site at Playa Vista.

An important resolution was finally honored at the Playa Vista project site against the 'Westchester Bluffs' near the Ballona Wetlands estuary and by the historic natural course of Ballona Creek.

At this location, the remains of the exhumed Tongva and other disinterred items; such as funerary objects and relics, are to be reinterred at a Tongva Historical Interpretive Center. The center is to be opened just off Lincoln Boulevard near the heart of the Playa Vista project.

Modern place-names with Tongva origins include: Pacoima, Tujunga, Topanga, Rancho Cucamonga, Azusa, and Cahuenga Pass.

The name of their creation deity, Quaoar, has been used to name a large object in the Kuiper belt, and their sky god, Weywot has been used for its satellite. A 2,656-foot summit in the Verdugo Mountains, in Glendale, has been named *Tongva Peak*. The *Gabrielino Trail* is a 28-mile path through the Angeles National Forest, (from *Wapedia*).

Every school child has read about or seen films depicting the great tug-of-war that existed between the European settlers of America and the great Native American Nations. Names like Iroquois, Apache, and Sioux, bring about blood-curdling images of torture and murder; on both sides.

It is important to note, that while our forefathers were waging the War of Independence with England, Southern California was already being colonized by the Spanish; at a place hardly accessible to most of the outside world. In fact, most maps of this time considered California an island.

So as the great Indian Nations waged war on the American Plains, the indigenous races of Southern California had already seen their ways of life changed forever. Curiously, there is very little recorded history documenting the Tongva/European struggle. This "forgotten time," is in need of illumination.

Gabrieliño traditional narratives or Tongva traditional narratives include myths, legends, tales, and oral histories preserved by the Tongva/Gabrieliño nation of people of the Los Angeles basin and vicinity in southern California. However, Tongva oral literature is relatively little known, because of the early (1770s) reduction of the people into the California Spanish mission culture, and their ruthless treatment and virtual enslavement.

It has been convenient to forget.

.

In 1542 Juan Cabrillo set anchor off of Playa Del Rey, near the tributary of what would one day be called the Los Angeles River. The Los Angeles River and dozens of smaller streams, and Centinela Springs, meandered through broad valleys to the sea. They carried so much fresh water to the sea that the Spanish explorer, could haul fresh water , (floating on seawater), aboard ship with a bucket.

Cabrillo was greeted by native Tongva, who rowed out in their canoes to greet him, but for reasons that no one is quite sure of, he upped anchor and moved north, and for over two hundred years the area remained the territory of native American tribes. They lived on the bluffs surrounded by a great alluvial plain.

The Spanish occupation began in 1769 with the Catalonian, Gaspar de Portola expedition, who with the Franciscan Friars, established Catholic Missions in the area; marking the beginning of the end of native peoples in the Los Angeles area Forced to give up their traditional lifestyle and exposed to disease, Native Americans both perished and deserted the area. By 1852, there were approximately 3,700 "domesticated" Indians and 4,000 Europeans in Southern California.

Portola was sent by the Viceroy of Mexico for another reason. As the newly appointed Governor of Baja California, he was responsible for expelling the Jesuit priests from Baja California where they had established 23 missions in 72 years. Beginning in 1633, under Father Eusebio Kino, and furthered by Father Juan Maria Salvatierra in 1635, Baja became the peninsula's religious and administrative capital.

Along with religion, the Jesuit explorer parties brought diseases that the native people had never been exposed to. By 1767 as Portola prepared to head north to Alta California, epidemics of smallpox, plague, typhus, measles and venereal diseases had decimated the population. Out of an initial population of about 48,000 only 8,000 still remained.

The Baja California missions were turned over to the Franciscans and later to the Dominicans, and the Upper-California Missions were expanded by the Franciscan Father Junipero Serra, all the way north through Alta California to present day San Francisco. Later, in 1770, Portola would be named Governor of all California. Mexico gained its independence in 1821 and in 1832 it began to put an end to the mission system by converting the missions into parish churches and disassembling the original Spanish Land Grants.

Mexican settlers divided the coastal plain into ranchos for cattle grazing and for crops like corn, beans, barley, and wheat. These ranchos bore names like Rancho Topanga, Malibu Sequit, Rancho Ballona, and Rancho San Vicente y Santa Monica. To support these farms, coastal scrub was converted to grassland through burning and grazing.

The rivers and streams that fed the *cienegas* or swamps were dammed and free-flowing watercourses were diked and channelized in crude ditches. Thus began the alteration of watercourses, the disappearance of wetlands, and the thwarting of sediment flows to replenish beach sands.

Rancho Centinela de Aguaje, which encompassed most if not all of modern day Westchester, Playa Vista, and Inglewood, CA, was carved out of the much larger Rancho Sausal Redondo (Ranch of the Circular Willow Grove, or Clump of Willows) which originally covered 22,458 acres.

In May 1846 President James K. Polk and America declared war on it's southern neighbor, Mexico. The path to war was slow, and it took a great amount of convincing for Congress to finally issue the Articles of War, for what would become nothing more than a dress rehearsal for our own Civil War.

Mexico had been in midst of a sustained political turmoil for over twenty years. During that time, eighteen rulers had led the country and the colony of California; and as was the case with the Mexican Army, it was generally undersupplied and overstaffed. Logistically, Mexico was hardly in a position to supply its army; the same conditions that would cause Spain and later France to lose its control of the Republic. In the end, the invading armies of the United States were no match for Mexico, and with the signing of the Treat of Guadalupe Hidalgo, California would become a possession of the Unites States. Then Brigadier General U.S. Grant summed up the Mexican War when he declared, "that the War was the most overmatched confrontation in modern history."

Years later Porfirio Diaz, the late 19th-century dictator, observed, "Poor Mexico, so far from God, but so close to the United States."

At any rate, the United States had become a continental nation, with Rancho Centinela near to the edge its extreme southwestern footprint.

Back at Westchester and Playa Del Rey, CA, the Machado brothers had already set up housekeeping on another man's land. Although their claims would later be validated, the occupation of Rancho La Ballona and Rancho Centinela was nothing short of good old fashioned land squatting.

The two ranchos had originally been one; the Rancho Sausal Redondo held by the Avila family, while the Rancho Centinela had been carved out of the Sausal Redondo by Ignacio Machado, member of another prominent *Californios* family, who had encroached on the Avila's' rancho, building at the springs there called the Aguaje de la Centinela.

Nine years before the outbreak of war; in 1837, the governor of California confirmed the Avila's' possession of the Rancho Sausal Redondo, while granting to Ignacio Machado provisional title to the Aguaje de la Centinela, also considered a rancho.

Bruno Avila would regain for his family the Aguaje de la Centinela from Machado in 1845 through an exchange of property in Los Angeles for the Rancho Centinela. At the eleventh hour, when Avila refused to sell his home on the Plaza Los Angeles, Machado sweetened the deal with a two, twenty gallon kegs of brandy, and the deed was signed. It may seem that Don Machado drank too much of his *aguardiente* before he made this transaction, which would be unbelievable by today's standards. But, at the time, a small house near the plaza of the pueblo was worth more than a remote 2,200-acre rancho with a house of equal size. So the trade was actually considered fair. All of this trading occurred just one year before the outbreak of the Mexican American War.

Highlighted from; *Historic Adobes of Southern California*, by John Kielbasa.

Bruno Avila moved into the Centinela adobe and went into the business of raising cattle on the land, which was adjacent to his brother's Rancho Sausal Redondo. Within ten years, Bruno accumulated several thousand head of cattle. After the Mexican War an influx of Americans came to California, especially after the Gold Rush of 1849. Bruno Avila found the American way of business to be extremely foreign to him, as did most Mexican landowners. Either due to necessity or improvidence, Avila on two separate occasions mortgaged his rancho. In 1854 he borrowed $400 from John G. Downey and agreed to pay six- percent interest per month, or seventy-two percent per year, which was the standard lending rate at the time for private loans. The following year he borrowed $1400 from Hilliard P. Dorsey , an American, at a similar interest rate. Avila, who put up Rancho La Centinela for collateral, was unable to repay the loans and subsequently lost his rancho in 1857.

The land was seized and auctioned off at a Sheriff's sale in Los Angeles. Hilliard P. Dorsey was the highest bidder and purchased the rancho for $2,000, or less than one dollar an acre. Dorsey was a veteran of the Mexican War. He was originally from the southern part of the United States and came to Los Angeles in 1853 where he pioneered in walnut cultivation. President Benjamin Pierce appointed Dorsey to register in the United States Land Commission Office in Los Angeles, a position he held until May 1857. Along with a group of prominent community leaders, he formed the first Masonic Lodge (#42) in Los Angeles and was the first "Worshipful Master" of the order on May 16, 1854.

Hilliard Dorsey was known throughout California as an individual with a fierce temper and was heralded as a gunslinger. Having several notches carved into his gun, they indicating all the kills credited to him. He was not a bad man with evil intentions; he was a man of extreme honor in a lawless time when dueling was a common method of protecting such honor.

In September 1854, Dorsey and Rasey Biven, a U.S. Indian Agent from Stockton, California, were involved in a physical altercation at the Bella Union Hotel in Los Angeles. The two men agreed to meet on the "Field of Honor" later that month in Oakland. The duel took place as agreed and both parties were injured by the first round of gunfire. Dorsey sustained a single wound to the abdomen and his opponent was struck in the left forearm.

They were stopped from inflicting more harm to each other by local authorities and were arrested. The charges were eventually dropped, but the incident caused Dorsey to be expelled from the Masons. The reason for expulsion was for engaging in a duel with a fellow Mason, namely Rasey Biven. The early 1850's had been difficult in many ways for Dorsey. His younger brother had been killed only a few years earlier by Indians in Mississippi and he was having foul marriage problems.

Dorsey's tumultuous disposition ultimately caused his untimely demise. He was married to a woman named Civility Rubbottom. Her father, William Rubbottom, settled in El Monte in 1853 and became one of the founders of the settlement of Spadra, near Pomona. Rubbottom was furious over Dorsey's poor treatment of his beloved daughter and the two became involved in a verbal dispute at Rubbottom's home in El Monte. The quarrel turned violent when Dorsey armed himself with a knife and pistol charged at his father-in-law. Rubbottom, in self-defense, shot and killed Dorsey.

After Dorsey's death in 1858, his widow, Civility, sold Rancho La Centinela at a mere thirty-five cents an acre. The total she received was $630, taking nearly a $1,500 loss. The buyer was a man named Francis J. Carpenter, who held the position of city jailer in Los Angeles in 1857. The drastic drop in the value of the property was due to an illegal squatter living there named Fernando Ayala. Fernando Ayala was the son-in-law of the prior owner, Bruno Avila. Ayala claimed that Avila gave him permission to settle on Rancho Centinela. A clause in Carpenter's deed stipulated that he, as part of the consideration, was to "run off and dispossess" Ayala . Carpenter was successful in evicting the squatter and that caused the value of the land to increase back to $1.00 an acre.

Today, many Southern California motorists who commute daily along the heavily traveled San Diego Freeway through southwestern Los Angeles are probably unaware they pass a hidden historic landmark. To the west of the freeway between the southbound exits of La Tijera and La Cienega Boulevards, a 176 year old adobe structure stands upon a bluff well concealed by a fence, trees and shrubbery. In the quiet residential neighborhood of Westchester, the adobe is a part of a small park located at 7634 Midfield Avenue.

Well-kept homes border the park to the north, south, and west. This modified adobe house does not show its age. Its shake roof and redwood-paneled outer wall covering seems to blend well with its modern residential surroundings. Driving past the front of the place, one would hardly notice this hidden historic site.

Known as the "Centinela Adobe", this ranch house is considered to be one of the most magnificently preserved smaller adobes in Los Angeles County. It was built in 1834 by Don Ignacio Machado and was the headquarters of over 25,000 acres of ranch land. The Centinela Adobe is considered the "Birthplace of Inglewood", the modern city which was formed upon the land grant known as "Rancho Aguaje de la Centinela". The old house and accompanying acreage passed through many hands over the years. One owner was of Scottish royalty and another was a Confederate General during the American Civil War.

Rancho Aguaje de la Centinela was formerly granted to Ignacio Machado in 1844. When translated, Aguaje de la Centinela means, "The Gathering Waters of the Sentinel". The area was named by early Spanish settlers at the beginning of the nineteenth century.

After the founding of the pueblo of Los Angeles in 1781, the townspeople used the area as public pastureland for their cattle. This prime grazing land was about eight miles southwest of the pueblo and only four miles east of Santa Monica Bay. This location made livestock extremely vulnerable to attack or theft of pirates and privateers who were pillaging the coast of Spanish California in the early nineteenth century.

The early settlers stationed sentinels in the area to guard the cattle. There was a hill in the vicinity, which the Spanish called "La Centinela". It had a commanding view of the Centinela Valley below. Bubbling springs, from a deep-water basin located 150 feet underground, began at the top of this hill. The Spanish named the springs "Aguaje de la Centinela" after the sentinel that stood guard upon the lonely hilltop.

**CENTINELA ADOBE, RANCHO CENTINELA, 1889.** (Complements, *Wikipedia*).

# The death of Hilliard Dorsey, December, 1865

*from; History OF POMONA VALLEY California with Biographical Sketches of The Leading Men and Women of the Valley -Who Have Been Identified With Its Growth and Development from the Early Days to the Present .*

By Frank Parkhurst Brackett, 1920. (Complements, Google Books).

When Dorsey learned that his wife and son had gone again to the Rubottom home in El Monte, he came down to the store and loaded his gun. "Better not go," said Burdick, "Uncle Billy is a desperate man and thinks nothing of killing.'"

But Dorsey replied, "Cy, I won't kill Uncle Billy," and went on his way. The old man saw his son-in-law coming along the hedge, by the path that led to the house, and he stood on the threshold to meet him. Love and honor were at stake with both. The father would defend his daughter; the husband would have his wife. Both were of Southern blood, fearless and unyielding. Both had fought to the death before.

It was Uncle Billy who called out, "Dorsey, you can not come in." And Dorsey, still advancing, said, "I'll have my wife or die in the attempt." "Stop," said Uncle Billy, "not another step."

But Dorsey, reaching up and plucking a leaf from the hedge, put the stem in his mouth and came steadily on, tossing Uncle Billy one of his brace of dueling pistols as he advanced.

At the same moment Uncle Billy reached for his shotgun and fired the fatal shot.

Friends of the family uphold them both. "It had to be," they said. "What else could either do?" But those who knew him best said that Uncle Billy always grieved for the man, and never ceased to regret.

The baby boy, his grandson, Kewen Dorsey, found his home with his grandfather until, sometime later, his mother was married again. And years after, the grandson cared for Uncle Billy in his declining years until his death.

---

**AUTHORS NOTE**: Following the death of Dorsey, curious happenings began to beset his heirs. Some say it was just bad luck, others say that the bad luck may have been helped along by Masonic brothers of Dorsey, unhappy over his death.

The abbreviated life of Civility Dorsey

Civility Rubottom Greenwade - (1840 - 1875) - daughter of William (Uncle Billy) Wiley Rubottom and Sarah Ann Edwards Rubottom.

-Marries Hilliard Dorsey - son is Kewen Dorsey.
-Hilliard Dorsey is killed by William Wiley Rubottom.
- Hilliard Dorsey's father tries to claim land deeds. Civility takes them back at gunpoint.

Civility later marries James M. Greenwade – they have a son Jeff Davis Greenwade, and daughter Elizabeth 'Lizzie' Greenwade.

January 1, 1869 - both James M. Greenwade and daughter Elizabeth die from accidental poisoning. Civility lives for only six years after all this.

She dies in 1875, the same year as her brother James R. Rubottom (1836 - Jan. 12, 1875), and his daughter, Inez Rubottom ( Sep 11 1868 - Dec 14 1875)

# Two

## THE GENERAL, THE SCOT, & THE CANUCK

Back at the Rancho, Carpenter immediately turned around and sold La Centinela for $3,000 to Joseph Lancaster Brent, one of the rancho's most illustrious owners. Brent was a southerner from Maryland and was a veteran of the Mexican War.  He had come around the Horn on a windjammer, and with him he brought the books that would comprise the first Los Angeles law library.

He came to Los Angeles in 1850 at age thirty and started a law practice. Don Ygnacio del Valle, owner of Rancho San Francisco, rented out two rooms of his home on the plaza to the young lawyer. The house on Los Angeles Street faced the plaza and was located next door to the Lugo family adobe. Brent used one of the rooms for his attorney's office and the other was for lodging.  Brent specialized in land law and became well known for his defense of rancheros against the annoying squatters, boundary disputes and other circumstances threatening their land claims. He often presented cases for the ranch owners in State and Federal Courts. Brent once told long time friend and fellow lawyer, James A. Watson; "Land was becoming the state's new gold rush. Opportunities were great for attorney's skilled in the intricacies of land law."

Watson married María Dolores Simona Dominguez, and founded Watson Land Co. The Dominguez Rancho was what is today is the entire Los Angeles harbor, the Palos Verdes peninsula, San Pedro, Redondo Beach, Hermosa Beach, Manhattan Beach, Torrance, Lomita, Harbor City, Wilmington, Carson, and Compton.

Brent's forecast of things to come eventually proved to be true. His law practice grew in leaps and bounds, enabling him to purchase his own ranchos, including La Centinela.

Brent represented many of the prominent and wealthy *Californio* families in their claims to land titles. He brought claims before the United States Land Commission on behalf of the Dominguez family of Rancho San Pedro, the Verdugos' of Rancho San Rafael, the Yorbas' of Rancho Santiago de Santa Ana, the Lugos' of Rancho San Antonio, Hugo Reid of Rancho Santa Anita and Pio Pico, who owned several ranchos.

Some of the old Dons or their heirs were unable to pay the costly legal fees and ended up giving Brent a portion of their land holdings in lieu of a cash payment. He also represented the pueblo of Los Angeles for the claim to the original pueblo lands consisting of 17,172 acres. He would receive $6,000 if the pueblo's claim was accepted by the District Court and an additional $3,000 if the claim was confirmed by the U.S. Supreme Court. The title for the original Pueblo de Los Angeles was confirmed in February 1856 and a United States Patent was secured on December 28, 1869.

Brent quickly established a good reputation and gained the trust of the Mexican landowners in Southern California when he tried one his first cases. In January 1851, two grandsons of Don Antonio Maria Lugo, the owner of Rancho San Antonio, were charged with a double murder.

They were accused of slaying two cattle rustlers whom they suspected of stealing stock from their father's Rancho San Bernardino. Brent, well versed in the area of jurisprudence, was able to obtain acquittals for the two teen-aged boys. He was paid $20,000 for his services by the Lugo family.

Joseph Brent was a man of versatility. Aside from his scholarly nature, he had a taste for adventure. He became a member of a group of hearty men known as the Rangers. The Rangers, led by A.W. Hope, were brave vigilantes who were armed, mounted and formed posses to search for dangerous fugitives on the run. The organization was comparable to the famous Texas Rangers.

Often their pursuits of desperate criminals led them through some rugged and unfriendly mountain and desert territory. Southern California in Joseph Brent's day, was every bit as wild and lawless as depicted in the old westerns created much later by Hollywood filmmakers. The Rangers were often the last line of defense against crime because organized law enforcement did not come about until the late 1860s.

Socially, Brent became quite active among the Californios. Often, he was invited to attend fiestas, balls, and fandangos. He related well with the Latino populace in and around Los Angeles. He befriended a business client, Manuel Dominguez, whose immense Rancho San Pedro south of the pueblo became one of his favorite retreats. He was equally sociable with his fellow Anglos who were newcomers to California. Like Hilliard P. Dorsey, he became a member of Lodge #42 of the Masonic Order.

Another one of Brent's talents was his flare for politics. He was a dedicated member of the Democratic Party. The Democrats formed a strong political foundation in Los Angeles in the 1850s and 1860s, especially among the Californios and the Americans from southern states. In July 1852, California's first Democratic Party convention was held in Benicia, in the northern part of the state. Brent attended and was selected as an alternate elector to cast a vote for Franklin Pierce, the Democrat candidate for the President of the United States. California electorates voted for Pierce in December 1852 and he became the nation's 14th President.

In the summer of 1853, Joseph Brent was appointed State School Commissioner. During the general election of September 1855, he was elected to the State Assembly as a Democrat from Los Angeles. He served on the Assembly until 1857. In 1856, he was selected as a delegate to attend the National Democratic Convention to support James Buchanan for President. Brent was such an influential power in California politics in the 1850s that he later credited himself by stating; "No one could be elected whom I did not support, and no one defeated whom I befriended". Brent could have had a promising political career if he continued, but he decided to pursue ranching and return to his lucrative law practice.

During the first year of his ownership of Rancho La Centinela, Brent was away at Washington, D.C.; working diligently to get all the land claims confirmed which he filed earlier in the decade.

He returned home to La Centinela in February 1859, but remained only a few years. Brent made another attempt at politics and was an influential force during the election of 1861.

That same year the nation was ripped apart by a bloody Civil War. The majority of Californians were in support of the Confederacy, especially Democrats. A subversive organization known as the Knights of the Golden Circle formed to get California to succeed from the Union and create an independent Pacific Republic. Organizers of the group approached Brent on several occasions asking him to lead them in their cause. He adamantly refused each time he was asked.

Brent, a Confederate sympathizer, felt that the best way to serve the Confederacy was to return to the South and assist their efforts first hand. Maintaining a professional obligation to his clients, Brent spent several weeks concluding all remaining business, including the sale of Rancho La Centinela.

When General Sumner of the Union army learned of Brent's plan to go and fight for the Confederacy, he intended to have him arrested for his disloyalty. Brent planned to board a New York bound steamship in San Francisco, jump ship along the way, and flee to a Southern controlled port. However, General Sumner had Brent arrested and imprisoned in New York. He was held captive for a short time and was soon released by an order from President Abraham Lincoln.

One account, states that Brent immediately went to New Orleans where he joined Confederate forces. By 1862, he achieved the rank of Brigadier General and served as an aid to General Robert E. Lee.

The account further states, he was in the company of Lee when the defeated old warrior surrendered to General Ulysses Grant at Appomattox Courthouse, Virginia on April 8, 1865. This event ended the American Civil War. After the war, Brent resided in Louisiana and eventually returned to his home state of Maryland.

As for this account, you can take it or leave that.

The next owner of Rancho La Centinela was a man of European nobility. Sir Robert Burnett was a Scottish baron from Crathes Castle, in Banchory, Scotland.

In the late 1850s, while touring California, he came upon the lands of La Centinela and was instantly attracted by its natural charm. Burnett purchased the rancho from Brent in 1860 for $3,000. It was the same price Brent paid for the property two years prior. Burnett and his wife, Lady Matilda Josephine Burnett, a native of New York, moved into the modest Centinela adobe.

It was quite a change in living standards, going from a Scottish Castle to a three room house of mud and straw, but Burnett put forth a great deal of effort into improving the casa and the surrounding ranch. His first improvement began with the second eviction of Fernando Ayala, the squatter who was first removed from the land by Francis Carpenter.

**CRATHES CASTLE.** 16th century castle near Banchory in the Aberdeenshire region of Scotland. This harled castle was built by the Burnett's of Leys and was held in that family for almost 400 years. The castle and grounds are presently owned and managed by the National Trust for Scotland and are open to the public. Crathes sits on land given as a gift to the Burnett of Leys family by King Robert the Bruce in 1323. *The Bruce* was featured in the Academy Award winning Mel Gibson film; *Braveheart.* (Complements, *Wikipedia*).

Evidently the persistent trespasser made another attempt to make La Centinela his home. After he was ousted by Burnett, Fernando Ayala returned to the pueblo where he found work as a tortilla maker. As time passed, Ayala grew discouraged with his life in California and returned to his native home in Sonora, Mexico.

Other enhancements contributed to the rancho by Burnett are the placement of wood shake roofing to the adobe and the covering of the dirt floor with one of wood. He built brick fireplaces and added a kitchen to the house. He may have been responsible for adding a second story to the south side of the adobe. Burnett constructed a windmill and began general cultivation of the surrounding area.

The nearby springs provided nourishment for Burnett's vegetable garden and vineyards. Sir Robert also bought the neighboring Rancho Sausal Redondo for $30,000, increasing his land holding to 25,000 acres. Burnett used the Sausal Redondo to raise sheep because the land there was considered too dry for farming. Burnett's flocks grew to an overwhelming 24,000 head.

The Burnett's were societal leaders and graciously entertained many important personalities at the Centinela adobe. But after thirteen years of the romantic rancho lifestyle in Southern California, the Burnett's decided to return to Scotland and to Crathes Castle following the death of Sir Robert's brother.

In 1969, Ms. Lila Fernyhough, a local historian,  visited one of Burnett's descendants at the old Scottish castle. During the visit she was given two original paintings of Sir Robert and brought them back to the United States. These portraits are currently on display at the Centinela adobe.

In 1873, Burnett leased his two ranchos to a Canadian born man named Daniel Freeman. The lease consideration was for $7,500 a year with the option to buy the properties. A further stipulation included that Freeman would have to carry out Burnett's original intention of planting thousands of various fruit trees.

Freeman was a lawyer who was born in 1837. He and his wife, Catherine Higginson Freeman, and their three children arrived in Southern California in 1873. They were attracted to the area after reading, "California, Land of Health, Pleasure and Residence", a popular book by Charles Nordhoff which contained positive features of the local environment.

The book described California's warm Mediterranean climate and Freeman figured it would be therapeutic for his wife who was in poor health, suffering from tuberculosis. Mrs. Freeman lived at the rancho for only a year and died in 1874.

Like Burnett before him, Freeman utilized the land for sheep ranching. It was a profitable business for a few years, but the drought of 1875-1876 brought on disastrous results. About 22,000 head of Freeman's sheep died in that period.

Looking for other means of income, Freeman attempted dry farming in 1875. He planted fields of wheat and barley, which turned out to be a wise move leading to financial success.

**THE DANIEL FREEMAN ESTATE; THE *CENTINELA*.** Freeman would eventually move from the adobe to this opulent estate. The location was on the 300 block of Prairie Avenue. (Complements, Google Books).

By 1880, Freeman was shipping a million bushels of grain a year to New York City and to Liverpool, England. At this time, over 22,000 acres of his property were under cultivation. On Rancho La Centinela, Freeman maintained vast orchards and raised horses, which he would periodically race along a trail that was to become Hillcrest Boulevard in Inglewood.

The Centinela adobe was the Freeman home and primary headquarters of his prosperous empire. In 1882, Freeman paid Sir Robert Burnett $22,243 for a portion of both ranchos. Later, with his business on a continuous upward trend, he was able to make a final payment of $140,000 in gold coin for acquisition of the combined 25,000 acres. Within twenty-five years the land increased in value from one dollar an acre to $4.25 an acre, leaving the Burnett's with a tremendous profit. The final papers for the sale of the two ranchos were signed in London on May 4, 1885 and Daniel Freeman officially became the owner of Rancho La Centinela.

## Peerage; and follow up on the life of; Sir Robert, and Lady Matilda Burnett of Leys

Arriving back in Scotland, Sir Robert Burnett assumed the life of a country gentleman. He would die only a few years after receiving full compensation for Rancho Centinela from Daniel Freeman, and left no male heir; his beloved son James, dying in 1874, one year after Sir Robert and Lady Matilda returned.

<u>Sir Robert Burnett of Leys, 11th Bt.</u>
b. 28 August 1833, d. 15 January 1894

> Sir Robert Burnett of Leys, 11th Bt. was born on 28 August 1833 at Edinburgh, Midlothian, Scotland. He was the son of Sir James Horn Burnett of Leys, 10th Bt. and Caroline Margaret Spearman. He married Matilda Josephine Murphy, daughter of James Murphy, on 23 May 1864.1 He died on 15 January 1894 at age 60 at Crossburn House, East Wemyss, Fife, Scotland, without surviving male issue.

> Sir Robert Burnett of Leys, 11th Bt. matriculated at Christ Church, Oxford University, Oxford, Oxfordshire, England, on 22 October 1851.3 He graduated from Christ Church, Oxford University, Oxford, Oxfordshire, England, in 1856 with a Bachelor of Arts (B.A.).3 He held the office of Deputy Lieutenant (D.L.) of Aberdeenshire.He held the office of Justice of the Peace (J.P.) for Aberdeenshire. He succeeded to the title of *11th Baronet Burnett, of Leys, co. Kincardine [N.S., 1626]* on 17 September 1876.

<u>Matilda Josephine Murphy</u>
d. 25 April 1888

Matilda Josephine Murphy was the daughter of James Murphy. She married Sir Robert Burnett of Leys, 11th Bt., son of Sir James Horn Burnett of Leys, 10th Bt. and Caroline Margaret Spearman, on 23 May 1864. She died on 25 April 1888.
From 23 May 1864, her married name became Burnett.

Child of Matilda Josephine Murphy and Sir Robert Burnett of Leys, 11th Bt. James Lauderdale Burnett
d. 1874

[S37] Charles Mosley, editor, *Burke's Peerage, Baronetage & Knightage, 107th edition, 3 volumes* (Wilmington, Delaware, U.S.A.: Burke's Peerage (Genealogical Books) Ltd, 2003), volume 1, page 593. Hereinafter cited as *Burke's Peerage and Baronetage, 107th edition*.(Complements, Peerage.com).

Cont.

## THE BURNETTS OF LEYS
### (The family tree can now be seen on Geni.com)

The Burnetts who went to the north east of Scotland did so after having been granted land there by the king, Robert the Bruce, for having supported him against Edward I of England in the War for Scottish Independence. In fact, the chief of this branch of the family, Alexander Burnard (Burnett) became an able and valued supporter of the Bruce and was rewarded with grants of part of the Royal Forest of Drum as well as neighbouring lands which had been forfeited by the Comyns.

As his badge of office as Royal Forester of Drum, Alexander was given the Horn of Leys.

### THE HORN OF LEYS.

On the lands to the north of the village of Banchory, there lay a stretch of shallow water known as the Loch of Banchory or the Loch of Leys. In the center of the loch was a crannog (artificial island), which had been a place of refuge for centuries. For the first 200 years of the Burnetts' residence in the area, this crannog provided the site for the family's principal stronghold. The loch is now drained and nothing remains but the island mound. The crannog may be deserted but the memory of the Burnetts' first home is kept alive in the traditional Scots territorial designation of the head of the family as "Burnett of Leys".

The crannog provided the Burnetts with security, and since the family was not politically ambitious, life was peaceful on the Loch of Leys.

The family spent most of its time in the pursuit of wealth and land, through judicious marriages and friendly relations with the church, in particular the Abbey of Arbroath, whose land covered much of the territory of Kincardineshire adjoining the Burnett estates. The Burnetts did not seem to have played much of a role in national affairs, preferring to keep their estates (and their lives) in hand.

However, the 4th Laird, Robert, became Deputy Sheriff of Kincardineshire and is believed to have fought for the King against the island rebels in one of the bloodiest and most savage encounters in Scottish history (The Battle of Harlaw Hill in July 1411). His son, Alexander, was rewarded with Banchory as a free barony by fighting for James I (who was murdered three months later).

In 1543 a marriage was arranged between the 9th Laird, another Alexander, and Janet Hamilton, the natural daughter of Canon Hamilton of the Abbey of Arbroath. As her dowry Janet brought a substantial amount of church lands. In later years, much land was added to Janet's dowry through arranged marriages and outright gifts. In 1560 Alexander and Janet decided that a better home was needed for their family, so the building of Crathes Castle began (taking 40 years). In 1563 Alexander fought for Mary, Queen of Scots, at the Battle of Corrichie.
Alexander's son and grandson both died in quick succession after him, so his great-grandson, also named Alexander, succeeded to the lands and was finally able to complete Crathes Castle. This Alexander was a most benevolent man who built a new church in Banchory and who gave much money to the poor.

Cont.

The next Laird, Thomas, succeeded his father in 1619 and was knighted by James VI. Charles I later made him a Baronet of Nova Scotia. Thomas' son had died as a child, so his grandson, another Alexander, was his successor. This Alexander was one of the few Burnett "black sheep". He was described at the age of sixteen as being "dissolute and naughty" and had managed to father at least 6 children by the time of his death at age 26. The 3rd Baronet, Sir Thomas, who with his wife Margaret produced 21 children in 22 years, was a member of the Scottish Parliament and after the Act of Union with England in 1707 was a member of the Westminster Parliament as well. Alexander, the 14th Laird and 4th Baronet, was mainly famous for refusing to join either of the Jacobite Risings of 1715 and 1745. (An interesting sidebar in regards to the "Forty-Five" is that Prince Charles Edward Stuart [Bonnie Prince Charlie] was sometimes referred to in cipher as "Mr. Burnett" during his time in Scotland). About 1746, a splinter of rock killed the 4th Baronet's son during the draining of the Loch of Leys. After that tragedy, Alexander developed a "boodie fear of beasties". In 1759, the 5th Baronet died unmarried and a seven-year battle between two rival Burnett cousins ensued. In the end, Thomas Burnett of Criggie won the legal battle for the title and Crathes Castle. His son Robert fought against the "rebels" in the American Revolutionary War and later became 7th Baronet. Three of Robert's sons succeeded to the title and all three died unmarried. Meanwhile, the heir to the title and the castle, Sir Robert, had immigrated to California where he was an extremely successful rancher. (He once owned half of the site of what was to become the city of Los Angeles). After marrying a New York woman, he returned to Crathes to become 11th Baronet. His son James had preceded him in death, so Sir Robert's brother, Colonel Thomas, succeeded as 12th Baronet.

Colonel Thomas' son Major General Sir James Lauderdale Gilbert Burnett of Leys became the 13th Baronet and was at one time the Commander of the Gordon Highlanders Regiment of the British Army. He was the last in residence at Crathes Castle.

The 13th Baronet's two sons, Alexander and Roger, both died as young men, so the estate passed through his daughter Elizabeth to her son James Cecil, who was obliged to change his surname to Burnett in order to succeed to the estate. The title of Baronet passes only through the male line, so the heir to the Baronetcy of Burnett of Leys is Alexander William Burnett Ramsay, who lives in Australia.

In 1952, the 13th Baronet gave Crathes Castle and a portion of the estate to the Scottish people, where it remains under the care of the National Trust for Scotland.

The current Laird, James Comyn Amherst Burnett of Leys and his family reside in the House of Crathes, a short distance from the Castle. His official title is "Representer of the House and Chief of the Name of Burnett of Leys"

The Burnett of Leys family (around 1993).

Cont.

*"Alterius Non Sit Qui Suus Esse Potest"*
(Let Him Not Be Another's Who Can Be His Own).

**SIR THOMAS BURNETT OF LEYS, First Baron of Leys, 1619-1653.** Sir Robert was the 11th Baron of Leys. (Courtesy, Burnett Family Archive, Scotland.)

**HENRY LAWRENCE  BURNETT** Brigadier-General,
Union Army, 1863. (Complements, Ancestry. COM).

On the surface, the wedding of Sir Robert Burnett to am American New Yorker;
Matilda Murphy, may seem unusual. In the 1850's it was rare to see a Scottish
Laird take an American wife.

But Sir Robert was not your normal Scotsman. He was a descendant of William
Burnet, colonial governor of New York, and a cousin of Henry Lawrence Burnett.

Henry L. Burnett, Union soldier and lawyer, was the son of Henry and Nancy Jones
Burnett, He was born at Youngstown, Ohio, December 26th, 1838. The Burnett
family -- or Burnet, as it has been frequently spelled -- is one of the oldest and
most honorable in the United States. More than one of it's family members  have
occupied positions of great importance in the history of the country. Burnett was
appointed to the Lincoln Assassination Court

A copy of General Burnett's memoirs on the Lincoln assassination begins, "I was
serving with my regiment, the 2nd Ohio Cavalry along the Cumberland in
Southern Kentucky in the latter part of the year 1863, when the Judge Advocate
on the staff of General Burnside, Major J. Madison Curtis (brother-in-law of the
late Senator Douglas), committed an offense for which charges were preferred
against him. General Burnside sent inquiries to the front for some officer who was
a lawyer, and who could be recommended as capable of trying his Judge
Advocate. I was recommended, and ordered back to Cincinnati, where General
Burnside's headquarters then were, as commander of the Department of the
Ohio. "

In September 1864, Burnett was ordered to Indiana to act as Judge Advocate of
the court detailed to try the members of the "Knights of the Golden Circle" or
"Sons of Liberty."  Shortly thereafter, he received a dispatch from the Secretary of
War, directing him to report in person immediately to the War Department to aid
in the examinations respecting the murder of President Lincoln and the
attempted assassination of Mr. Seward.

THE ASSASSINATION OF PRESIDENT LINCOLN.
AT FORD'S THEATRE WASHINGTON D.C APRIL 14TH 1865.

**BURNETT MEMOIR.** "The execution of the assassins was the closing scene of the greatest tragedy in our history. The assassination removed from the stage of life the greatest figure of the century. " Note: On July 7, 1865, forty-two-year-old Mary Surratt, an attractive, dark-haired widow, was hanged on the gallows at the Old Arsenal Penitentiary in Washington along with three others convicted of complicity in the assassination of Abraham Lincoln. (Complements, Ancestry. COM).

**LINCOLN ASSISINATION MILITARY COURT.** The detail of the "Court was as follows: Major-General David Hunter, Major-General Lewis Wallace, Brevet Major-General Augustus V. Kautz, Brigadier-General Albion P. Howe, Brigadier-General Albert S. Foster, Brigadier-General T.M. Harris, Brevet Brigadier-General James A. Ekin, Colonel C.H. Tompkins, Lieutenant-Colonel David T. Clendenin. Brigadier-General Joseph Holt was appointed Judge Advocate and recorder of the commission, and the Honorable A. Bingham and myself were assigned as assistants or special Judge advocates"-**Burnett's memoir.** (Complements, Ancestry. COM).

**DOWNTOWN LOS ANGELES, 1873.** The land booms of the 1880's and the period from 1910 to 1929, would change the face of the region forever, as the city of Los Angeles, and nearby cities and towns such as Inglewood and Port Ballona, began to shift from a primarily agrarian economy to an industrial economy. There was a widespread change in how people worked and how they lived and how they created value to the economy. It was accompanied by a great social transformation; such as the reorganization of families, great migrations to the cities and co-dependency, (workers and industrialists depended on each other, where farmers were relatively self-sufficient). As can be seen in the above photo/postcard, farming was a main interest in Downtown Los Angeles well into the late 1800's. In fact, the first lots sold, creating the town of Westchester, CA, were sold as farms. (Complements, United States Library of Congress).

Again, back at the Rancho; The Centinela Valley remained sparsely settled for several years with the exception of a few tenant farmers and Freeman's ranch hands. The Land Boom of the 1880s in Los Angeles County changed the profile of the valley drastically.

Promoters from Los Angeles sought the potential for land development and wanted to plat a town site near Centinela Springs. In 1887, the Centinela-Inglewood Land Company was formed and began surveying the two ranches belonging to Daniel Freeman in August of that year. Freeman, interested in the long-term plans of the organization, sold 11,000 acres of his prime orchard land to the company at $1.25 an acre. This tract was to become the city of Inglewood.

The Centinela-Inglewood Land Company initially named the development Centinela Colony. They divided parcels of land into 20, 40, 80 and 160-acre plots. Residential lots were priced between $200 and $750 a piece. Farmland was offered at $200 to $400 an acre, and fine orchard property was listed between $600 to $1500 per acre. Centinela Colony was one of the most successful of the land boom subdivisions with the developers procuring over $1,000,000 in capital by 1888. In the first year of its existence, the incredible amount of $20,000 was spent for advertising alone.

Local real estate moguls of the era were among the Board of Directors of the land company including: Dan McFarland, Edward C. Webster, L.T. Garnsey and Leonard J. Rose, the founder of Rosemead, California.

In 1887 a railroad was completed linking Los Angeles to Santa Monica Bay. This line was constructed by California Central Railroad (forerunner of Atchinson, Topeka and Santa Fe) and coursed through the center of Freeman's ranchos. Known as the Los Angeles and Ballona Branch, it had a depot built at Centinela Colony. Another rail line was extended to Redondo Beach from the Centinela Station. In 1888, the Centinela-Inglewood Land Company merged with land promoters from Redondo and reorganized under the name of Redondo Beach and Centinela-Inglewood Land Company.

By 1888, all lots for the young town were occupied and two business blocks were completed. The name of the town was changed from Centinela to "Inglewood", named for Daniel Freeman's Canadian hometown. Construction was underway for a stately, elegant hotel. One of Freeman's barns was used as one of the first schools in Inglewood. Population of the town was 300 at the Boom's peak in 1888. Plans for a college of applied sciences, with emphasis in farming and agriculture was in the making. The college was to be operated by the University of Southern California (USC). Daniel Freeman donated $600,000 to the University, with $100,000 of it designated for construction of the buildings.

When Freeman designed the Inglewood plat, he selected for himself sixty acres near Centinela Springs to be used as his new manor. He started building a grand three-story Victorian mansion on the site in 1888. It was completed the following year.

When finished, the Freeman's left the primitive Centinela adobe to occupy their new lavish home. The site of the Freeman mansion was at 333 N. Prairie Avenue, Inglewood. The old adobe served as the residence of Freeman's ranch manager until 1912.

In 1889, a huge financial crash brought an end to the Great Land Boom. The collapse proved devastating for most real estate developments in Southern California and some towns were propelled into oblivion. Inglewood fared better than most, but still felt the harmful effects.

The newly completed hotel went bankrupt without it ever being furnished and plans for Daniel Freeman's college were scrapped permanently. In 1890, Freeman repossessed all lots that the land company was unable to sell, yet the town of Inglewood survived and continued to grow. It incorporated as a city in 1908 with a population of 1,200. From 1920 to 1925, Inglewood was the fastest growing city in the United States.

Daniel Freeman continued selling town lots until 1912, when the Los Angeles Extension Company purchased the last 4,000 acres surrounding the old adobe. The company proceeded to subdivide the land into small farms available for lease. Eventually this area evolved into the community of Westchester and was annexed to the city of Los Angeles on June 16, 1917. During this period the Centinela adobe was transformed from a home into an exclusive riding academy.

Daniel Freeman was a multi-faceted individual; being a lawyer, farmer, rancher, educator, land developer, businessman and philanthropist. Freeman, "The Father of Inglewood", died on September 28, 1918 in the town he founded thirty years earlier. His daughter, Grace Freeman Howland, who spent her childhood at the Centinela adobe, lived in the Freeman Mansion on Prairie Avenue until her own death in 1956.

She donated land near the home where the Daniel Freeman Memorial Hospital was built. Near the hospital grounds are Grace Avenue and Howland Drive, named in honor of Mrs. Howland.

Unbelievably, the Freeman Mansion was demolished in 1972.

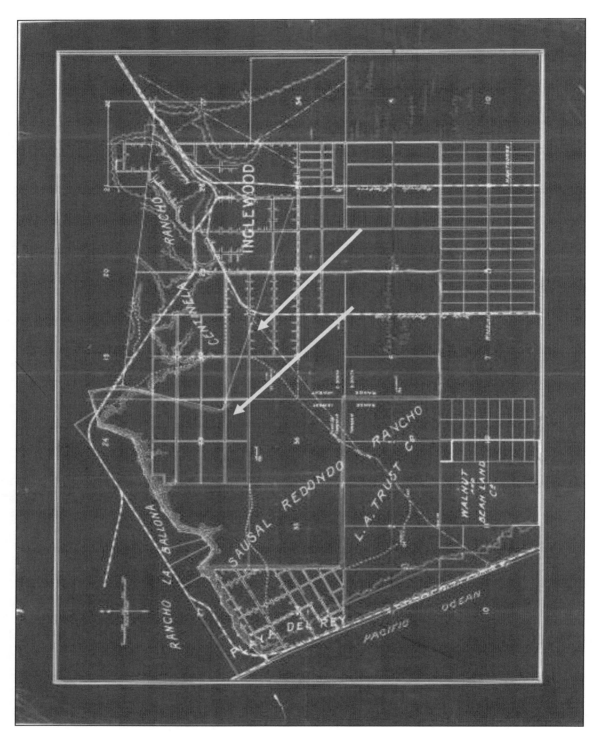

**1912 SUBDIVISION**. Freemen sold 4000 acres of his Centinela Rancho to Los Angeles Extension Company creating what would one day be know as Westchester. Other parts of the original Rancho Sausal Redondo were rapidly being developed as well, creating towns such as of Playa Del Rey, Hawthorne and Gardena. Arrows; west and east Westchester. (Complements, Los Angeles Public Library).

In 1923, Martha Crawford, the wife of a Los Angeles Extension Company executive, Charles Crawford, moved into the adobe with their two children. For 25 years, Mrs. Crawford resided here and maintained the aged structure. The east side of the house was used as the main entrance.

It was Charles Crawford who named the town of Westchester, probably named for the County in New York, although some say he named the town after an automobile.

Prior to construction of the freeway, the adobe was accessible from Redondo Beach Boulevard; The Old Port Road, (now Florence Avenue) via a long private driveway aligned with flowers and trees.

During her occupation of the place, Mrs. Crawford operated a nursery school here and opened the house to the public periodically, hosting several small social events. In 1937, she had the Centinela adobe placed in the National Register of Historic Places and recorded in the Library of Congress.

In 1949, Martha Crawford vacated the adobe and the casa was subsequently rented to a succession of families. The ensuing years left the adobe dwelling in a tragic state of disrepair, until a group of local residents purchased the building in 1950.

This group, known as La Casa de la Centinela Adobe Association, began restoration efforts. They plastered the inside walls and applied a stucco coating over exposed adobe brick outside. The old roof was replaced with a wood shake roof, replicating the one that existed during the Burnett ownership. The Association received numerous donations of Victorian era furnishings to fill the rooms of the house.

The Centinela adobe was deeded to the city of Inglewood in 1956 and was maintained by the Inglewood Department of Parks and Recreation, although the property is actually within the city limits of Los Angeles and the town of Westchester. The old adobe is important to Inglewood and is recognized as the birthplace of the city. In 1965, the Centinela Adobe Association joined with the Historical Society of Centinela Valley.

The organization provided the adobe with volunteer resident docents to keep it open to the public as a historic showplace. Today the Centinela adobe is managed by the historical society and still maintained by the Inglewood Parks and Recreation Department. I

It is open to the public for tours. For history buffs, it is a remarkable site to be explored.

**POSTCARD, RANCHO CENTINELA AGUAJE, WESTCHESTER, CA.**
Freeman amassed a fortune farming barley, olives, grapes, lemons, limes and almonds on the ranch, and named his expansive land holding Inglewood, after his birthplace in Ontario; an area today called Caledon. Caledon is somewhat urban, though it is primarily rural in nature. Many of Toronto's wealthiest citizens own large country estates in the area, among them many members of the Eaton Family, Norman Jewison, and the inventors of the board game Trivial Pursuit. It consists of an amalgamation of a number of urban areas, villages, and hamlets; its major urban centre is Bolton, located on its eastern side adjacent to York Region. Tours of the adobe are free to the public. (Complements, Authors Collection).

**DANIEL FREEMAN LAND OFFICE.** The Freeman Land Office, built in 1887 for the Centinela-Inglewood Land Company and originally located on Florence Avenue east of Eucalyptus Avenue, and is also accessible as part of the tours. The grounds also include a heritage and research center which opened in 1980. The research center houses items from the Daniel Freeman mansion, which was demolished in 1972. Items on display in the research center include Freeman's library, safe, and furniture, as well as articles and photos about the history of Centinela Valley. (Complements, *Wikipedia*).

**BRIGADEER GENERAL BRENT, 1880, Baltimore, MD.** (Complements, Google Books). He was a pioneer attorney and one of the first Americans to own land in what is now called Glendale. Between 1855 and 1858, Brent purchased a portion of Rancho San Rafael, adding up to 671 acres, from Julio and his sister Catalina Verdugo. The land was located across from the Los Angeles River, at what is now known as Griffith Park. . He named his property Santa Eulalia Ranch; named for a martyred Christian Saint. After selling his Rancho's, including Rancho Centinela, he joined the Confederate Army and was promoted to Brigadier General and given command of a Louisiana cavalry brigade on April 17th, 1864, becoming the only California citizen to become a Confederate General. Joe Brent never returned to California, and lived his days out in Louisiana and Maryland. Daniel Freeman would later own the Rancho and subdivide it, creating Westchester and Inglewood, CA. (Complements, findagrave.com).

**BRENT TOMBSTONE**, 1826-1905. Green Mount Cemetery, Baltimore, Maryland.

**RANCHO CENTINELA, WESTCHESTER, CA, 1889.** View from the Rancho Aguaje de la Centinela adobe house looking northeast over what is now the San Diego freeway. (Courtesy, LAPL).

**WILLIAM STARKE ROSECRANS, LEFT, IN A PORTRAIT BY PRICE, & RIGHT, IN A PHOTOGRAPH BY MATHEW BRADY.**

Doomed from the start, the Rancho system rapidly fell apart after the defeat of Mexico in the Mexican-American War. The once grand Rancho Sausal Redondo was divided time and time again, and the portion that today we call Gardena and Hawthorne, CA, was purchased by General William Starke Rosecrans, in 1869. General Rosecrans bought 16,000 acres of Rancho San Pedro in the Los Angeles basin for $2.50 an acre, a low price possibly because the land was deemed worthless for lack of a spring for water. The ranch, dubbed "Rosecrans Rancho", was bordered by what later was roughly Florence Avenue on the north, Redondo Beach Boulevard on the south, Central Avenue on the east, and Arlington Avenue on the west; effectively most of present day Hawthorne and Gardena, CA; and parts of Redondo Beach and Inglewood.

**GENERAL ROSECRANS, SHORTLY BEFORE HIS DEATH IN 1898.**

He gained fame for his role as a Union general during the American Civil War. He was the victor at prominent Western Theater battles such as Second Corinth, Stones River, and the Tullahoma Campaign, but his military career was effectively ended following his disastrous defeat at the Battle of Chickamauga in 1863. (Photos; Complements, the Army of Northern Virginia, and *Wikipedia*.)

45

Rosecrans Pioneer Homestead, Rosecrans Ave., Los Angeles, California.    Built 1873-Rebuilt 1895.

**POSTCARD, ROSECRANS RANCHO, GARDENA, CA.** The Rosecrans Homestead was torn down in 1950. It was located at the present day intersection of Vermont and Rosecrans Avenues, in Gardena, CA.  Rosecrans died at his Rancho and lay in state in Los Angeles City Hall. In 1908 his remains were re-interred in Arlington National Cemetery. Fort Rosecrans National Cemetery, in San Diego, California is named in his honor, as is Rosecrans Avenue, a major east-west street that runs through the southern part of Los Angeles County. It turned out that there was water on his land, and along with his neighbor Daniel Freeman, Rosecrans shipped his abundant crops from the onetime wharf and seaport at Port Ballona, CA; now called Playa Del Rey, utilizing the SANTA FE & SANTA MONICA RAILWAY COMPANY, Incorporated  April 4, 1892. The tracks ran from near Mesmer Station, on the line of the Southern California Railway, between Inglewood and Ballona, to the town of Santa Monica. (Complements, Google Books).

**1901, BEAN FIELD.** Below the bluffs in Westchester, workers harvesting the field. (Courtesy, Google).

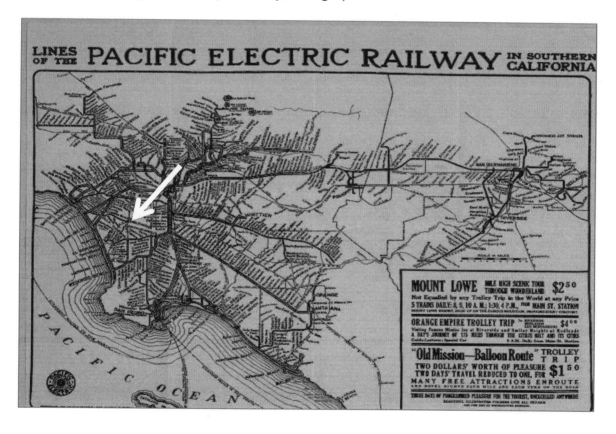

**INGLEWOOD RAIL TERMINUS**. In many respects, the Inglewood/Redondo/Santa Monica junctions were critical for the distribution of people and goods to the early Westside of Los Angeles. (Complements, Los Angeles Public Library).

**DANIEL FREEMAN, (1837-1918).** The founder of Inglewood. He was born in 1837, on a farm in the province of Ontario, Canada. Once his wife contracted tuberculosis, the family moved to Julian, California. After some time here in California, Freeman came to own two former Spanish ranchos, Rancho Centinela and Rancho Sausal Redondo, which he later developed, first raising sheep and later raised grain. His large land holdings helped make him a prominent businessman, whose reputation in the Los Angeles business community earned him the presidency of the Los Angeles Chamber of Commerce, (1893-1894). He also served as director of the Southern California Railway and was an esteemed benefactor of the University of Southern California. A hospital in Inglewood, the Daniel Freeman Memorial Hospital, was named after him. (Courtesy, LAPL).

**1871 MAP.** This 1871 map lists the area of Westchester and Inglewood as **FLORENCE, CA.** Port Ballona of RANCHO **BALLONA** first appeared here on the map. (Complements, United States Library of Congress).

**INGLEWOOD, CA POST OFFICE.** Influenced by Charles Nordhoff's "California for Health, Pleasure and Residence: A Book for Travelers and Settlers," Daniel Freeman settled in Centinela Ranch, where he felt the cool sea breeze would benefit his wife's poor health. There he built a vast empire through dry farming, shipping millions of bushels of barley from his wharf at Playa del Rey. Inglewood was the first settlement to be carved out of the 25,000 acre Centinela Ranch in 1888 shortly after a railroad station had been built in the area. The new town of 300 residents opened the first day of school, May 21, of that same year, enrolling 33 children in a new livery stable until the school building could be erected. Town politics also began in 1888 when F.B. Mitchell was appointed deputy county clerk and A.M. Rollins was sworn in as deputy sheriff after the town's ornamental cannon had been blown to bits in a prank. In 1905, Inglewood recovered from a nationwide financial crash after establishing a Poultry Colony in the present North Inglewood. Inglewood Park Cemetery was developed and the street car line brought both coffins and mourners. (Courtesy, City of Inglewood).

**DANIEL FREEMAN RESIDENCE, INGLEWOOD, CA, 1893.**
(Courtesy, LAPL).

**WINDMILL, DANIEL FREEMAN RESIDENCE, INGLEWOOD, CA, 1891.** This is a view of the Centinela Valley looking northwest. (Courtesy, LAPL).

**DANIEL FREEMAN, 1902**. (Courtesy, LAPL).

**LOS ANGELES PACIFIC RED CAR, 1904.** All of the Westside of Los Angeles; Inglewood, Port Ballona( renamed Playa del Rey), Santa Monica, and Redondo, were serviced by the Red Cars. Passengers and freight arriving from the East via rail, or by tall-ship, were widely distributed via Red Cars throughout the region. Shipping piers dotted the coastline from Malibu to Redondo Beach. This is a view of the freight and passenger depot at Hermosa Beach Pier; next stop; Port Redondo. (Complements, LAPL).

Casino (looking from beach), Playa del Rey, California

**POSTCARD VIEW; "CASINO," PLAYA DEL REY, 1904.** Very rare view of the Playa Del Rey Pavilion from the Playa Del Rey Pier. Mount Ballona; rises in the background, as diners watch visitors on the beach. (Courtesy, Author).

**FREEMAN RESIDENCE, & DOWNTOWN INGLEWOOD.** Inglewood, California, 1910. The bottom view is of Commercial Street, later a part of La Brea Avenue. (Complements, Google Books).

**SUNSET, CA, 1887.** As Rancho Centinela was subdivided, a new town just north was created at the former Rancho San Jose de Buenos Ayres.; Sunset, CA., but the town was never built. Today we know this area as Westwood, Bel Air and parts of West Los Angeles. The land was later owned by Arthur Letts, the founder of the Broadway Department Store chain. (Complements, United States Library of Congress).

**DANIEL FREEMAN, (1837-1918).** Below, another view of the Freeman Mansion, The Centinela. An innovator in many ways, he would subdivide property, sell the lots, and then sell the purchaser lumber and supplies; including building bricks from his own brick-yard. *Authors note*: Daniel Freeman; "Father of Inglewood," had emigrated from Simcoe, Ontario, Canada, and was a close friend and one time neighbor of my Canadian great-grandfather, William Crawford Thompson. (Complements, Google).

**BURDETT/DYCER AIRPORT, INGLEWOOD.** The Airport located at 33.95 North / 118.31 West , at 94th & Western Avenue, was first operated by Burdette Fuller & was called Burdette Field. Burdette Field was home to the famous stunt team "The Black Cats". The Black Cats were a company of flamboyant Los Angeles-based stunt pilots who defied both superstition & the odds on survival at Burdette Airport in the 1920's.Lots of footage was taken of the black cats doing various stunts, and the footage appeared in many movies. The black cats were involved with motion pictures & received a lot of publicity. The Burdette School of Aviation was established in 1925 by Burdette Fuller & Jack Frye as a base for Burdette Airlines. Fuller sold the field to Jack Frye, who founded Aero Corp, which became TWA. Burdette Fuller taught Frye how to fly. After Frye left, Charles Dycer bought the field. (Complements, University of California).

**DYCER AIRPORT, 1929, LOOKING WEST TOWARDS INGLEWOOD.**
(Complements, University of California).

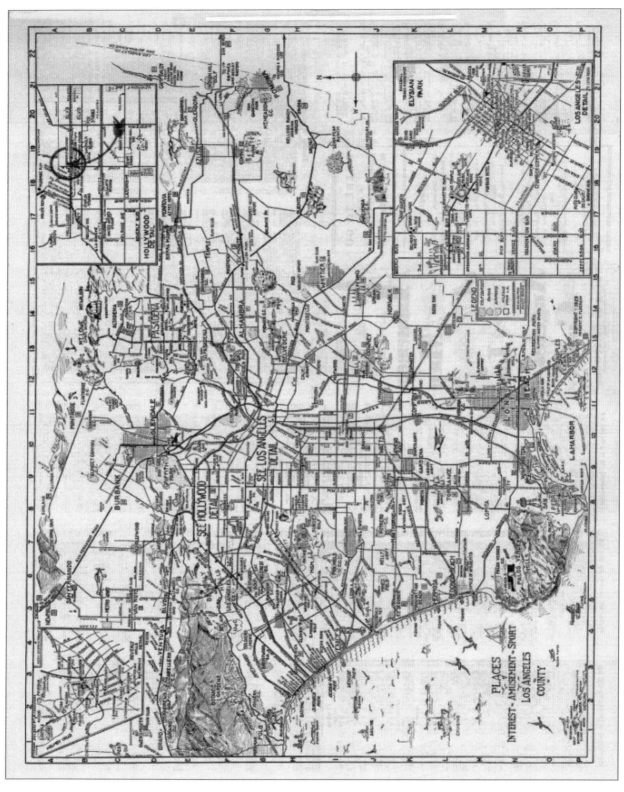

**MAP, 1929**. Amusement Map of Los Angeles County, 1929. (Courtesy, LAPL).

# *Three*
## *ROARING TWENTIES-DESPERATE THIRTIES*

With the passing of Daniel Freeman in 1918, and the ongoing subdivision of Augustine Machado's Rancho La Ballona and the Avila/Machado's Rancho Centinela, the connection to the Rancho Days of California were all but forgotten.

The arrival of the European to the area, had assured the annihilation of indigenous groups as well as many of the early Mexican settlers. What was not destroyed in the name of the Father; another mission; one driven by O'Sullivan's *Manifest Destiny*, would complete the deed, nearly erasing the tribes from the face of the planet.

The La Ballona Rancho existed, but only for five or six decades, sustained primarily through cattle ranching and farming. In fact, parts of the area was a vibrant farming community well into the 1970's. It also was , through a lease agreement with the City of Los Angeles, the depository for most of the populations raw sewage .

An Alsatian by the name of André Briswalter pursued farming and sold his vegetables door to door with a horse and wagon. The growth and success of his business allowed him to purchase vast tracts of land, including much of what is today known as Playa Vista and Westchester; below the Bluffs.

Briswalter had purchased the land and created a giant leech field or "sewer farm" on the Ballona Wetlands; the muck carried by pipes from Downtown Los Angeles, over the *Lucky* Baldwin Hills, and finally released onto the open ground. What was not recycled in this manner, generally washed down from the hills and to the Pacific Ocean via Ballona Creek; the former route of the Los Angeles River.

Further development of the Sausal Redondo created the new cities of El Segundo, Hermosa Beach, and Manhattan Beach; and up from the ashes, a new attempt to develop the Del Rey Hills and Palisades Del Rey began in earnest. Joseph Brent's prediction, that, "Land was becoming the state's new gold rush," would more than ever before prove to be true.

Where once only cattle trails, wagon roads and cultivated acreage existed, the area was now dotted with railroad and trolley tracks, automobile roads and a thing called an "airport,"; a new term which had first appeared in a *New York Times* article in 1902, where reporter Alberto Santos-Dumont stated that "he expected New York to be the principal 'airport' of the world in less than a score of years".

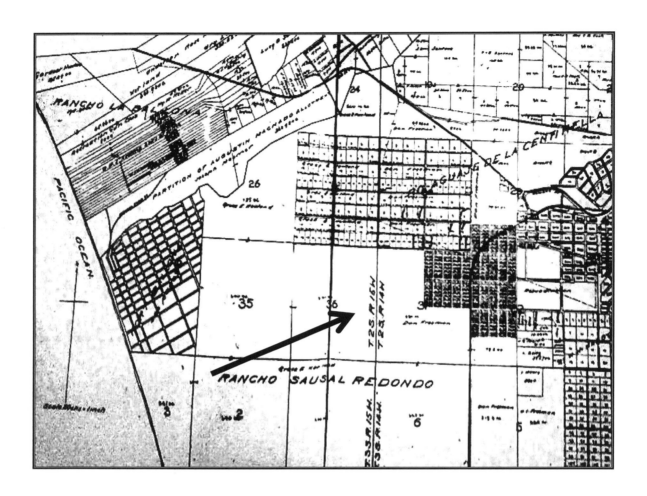

**HENRY REUGER MAP, RANCHO'S; LA BALLONA, CENTINELA AND SAUSAL REDONDO, 1903.** One of the earliest "modern" maps of Westchester, Playa Del Rey and Inglewood. The area simply names the future Westchester and Del Rey Hills as; Rancho Sausal Redondo. Henry Reuger was one of the earliest publishers of wall maps and made an atlas of the Los Angeles area. The map appears to be an updated version of the *1902 Maps of Greater Los Angeles*. At this point, Daniel Freeman owned all of Westchester. (Complements, Author's private collection).

A few decades before, Port Ballona had been an attempt to locate a new harbor for the city of Los Angeles, and when that failed, the area was reduced to a worthless slough. With the advent of the Los Angeles Pacific trolleys cars, and later mass production of the automobile, easy access to the hinterlands of Los Angeles created an opportunity to develop the new town, renamed ; Playa del Rey. The Beach Land Company and the interests of Moses Sherman would spark this development, including a new seaside resort; pier and pavilion. The Beach Land effort did produce a few permanent residents, but for the most part these activities burned to the ground and were washed into the sea; including the "Mammoth" Pleasure Pavilion, fishing pier, boat racecourse, lagoon hotel, and many fond memories. Even the Bank of Playa Del Rey and the U.S. Post Office closed their doors.

In the 1920's, a Minneapolis group called Dickinson and Gillespie began to redevelop the area adjacent to the Lagoon, and renamed it Palisades Del Rey, Surfridge and Del Rey Hills. Weekly newspapers and worldwide advertising heralded the area as, "The Last of the Beaches". Other developers and speculators soon joined the effort.

Trolley service and improved automobile roads buoyed these efforts, and the successful tourist enterprises of Venice, CA helped to keep interest up in the area, as did the later development of the Bennet Brothers farm which created a new airport for Los Angeles; Mine's Field. In 1928, the airport would host the National Air Races. Grassy landing fields were replaced; fittingly in this case, with adobe runways.

The Del Rey Hills, platted east of the Del Rey Lagoon area and on the Bluffs, and then heading south to Mines Field, would be the last of the area where development began, just before the Stock Market Crash of 1929.

But even the determination of D and G's new phenom; Fritz Burns, could not hold back the tide of debt and discourse in a Nation thrown into Depression. The broke and nearly despaired Burns would even lose his stately mansion to foreclosure, and move into a housekeeping tent on the dunes of what is today called, Toe's Beach. The entire enterprise had failed in less than ten years.

Another real estate entrepreneur, and said to have sold the first lot at Palisades Del Rey, T.O. McCoye opened his own real estate office, as well as converting the old bank building into the Del Rey Cooperative Market, trading staples and supplies to local farmers in exchange for fresh produce. Tom Lieb, the newly installed coach of Loyola's Fighting Lions football and hockey teams, would open a service station down the street.

Trying to rally his resources, Burns purchased the abandoned male dormitories from the 1932 Los Angeles Olympiad's Olympic Village in Baldwin Hills, and moved them to the current location of Toe's Beach as bath houses, renaming it Olympic Beach. The 1932 Summer Olympics were a financial disaster. Fewer than half the participants of the 1928 Summer Olympics in Amsterdam returned to compete in 1932. U.S. President Herbert Hoover did not attend the Games, becoming the first sitting head of government not to appear at an Olympics hosted in that country. They were selling anything they could to try and recoup the losses. The cross-country equestrian events were held at Westchester.

A few years before, in May 1927, Fritz Burns, Justin Dickinson, Clifford Gillespie and Bill Schreyer; all officers of Dickinson and Gillespie, persuaded Harry Culver, founder of nearby Culver City, to create a consortium called the Blankenthorn Syndicate, and to donate eighty acres to build a Lutheran College on the Del Rey Hills. Burns and Company donated another twenty acres of land to give the university an even one hundred acres to build on. This land was directly west of Lincoln Boulevard.

While they no doubt had a very high level of civic pride and altruistic intents, the building of a university in the area would spark further growth and increase real estate prices. Shortly thereafter, Culver donated another one hundred acres to the Society of Jesus to build still another university. This land was directly east of Lincoln Boulevard.

The Jesuit University, Loyola University opened on the Del Rey Hills in 1929. With the exception of the University, a few homes and ramshackle farm houses, none of what we know today as Westchester existed. The entire area in those days was dedicated to farming. The Los Angeles Lutheran College would never be built.

In 1931 The weather was strange as record temperatures hovered around the 100 degree mark throughout the summer. Ocean temperatures reached between 76 and 78 degrees and hammerhead sharks were sighted in bay for the first time. It was so hot in Los Angeles on July 26th that 350,000 people fled to the beach between Del Rey to the Ocean Park Pier. Thousands camped out on the beach at night, discovered the ideal weather, and many moved here for good.

Back at Del Rey, and as income from the new bath houses and cottages that Fritz Burns had established at Olympic Beach in 1933 began to flow in, Burns was able to pay off some pesky creditors, including the U.S .Government who he owed a massive tax debt.  With  just a few other pieces of rental property and useless deeds along the Del Rey Hills, Burns enlisted the Herndon Oil Company to prospect for oil on his properties . In the event of an oil strike, Burns would receive two percent of the proceeds.

*They Saw the Possibilities—this is what Manchester Boulevard leading to Loyola University looked like in 1928, the year construction began on the Westchester campus.*

**MANCHESTER BOULEVARD, WESTCHESTER, CA,  MAY, 1928.** Looking west  from about Emerson Avenue . (Courtesy, Google Books).

The region that had turned  so many souls from fortune to devastation  paid off for Burns when in October 1934 an oil gusher was tapped on his land at Delganey Avenue and Manchester Boulevard. The well soon began producing over fifty thousand dollars a month in income, and over one thousand dollars a month to Burns.

Burns was back.

By the late 1930's the region had begun to stabilize from the effects of the Depression, and some permanent residential development had been sustained.

Streets had been paved and sewers modernized; business's to support the new areas of Playa Del Rey and **University Studio Center** (Westchester),   sprung up all over. Markets, laundries, restaurants, diners, gas stations, florists, liquor stores, car dealerships and every other form of enterprise to support the residents of the area were opened.  Police and Fire stations were established close by.

The name; University Studio Center, was a neologism for Loyola **University**, and Harry Culver's nearby **Studio** interests in Culver City, and is generally attributed to Fritz Burns.

Farms still covered most of  the Westchester landscape, and with that enterprise came some other benefits. The area remained virtually unaffected by the Volstead Act and he National Prohibition,  as over 80% of local farmers made some sort of home brew, wine or distilled spirits. Of course, these practices had been taking place since the days of the Spanish Rancho's, and brewing, wine making, and distilling techniques were common knowledge to the modern day farmers. You could not legally order a drink out at a dinner-house, but libations flowed freely at home, and many gentlemen carried a pocket-flask, enjoying the potent portable potable for a night out on the town. In fact, Alcohol consumption rose to record levels during alcohol prohibition, all over America,  and the residents of this town did their parts to help it.

Also, large numbers of people began making their own alcoholic beverages at home. To do so, they often used bricks of wine, sometimes called blocks of wine. To meet the booming demand for grape juice, California grape growers; some cultivated right here in town and just north in nearby Malibu, increased their area about 700% in the first five years of prohibition. The juice was commonly sold as "bricks or blocks of Rhine  wine, or blocks of port," and sold  along with a warning:

*"After dissolving the brick in a gallon of water, do not place the liquid in a jug away in the cupboard for twenty days, because then it would turn into wine."*

Mines Field was dedicated and opened as the official airport of Los Angeles in 1930, and the city purchased it to be a municipal airfield in 1937. The name was officially changed to Los Angeles Airport in 1941, (and to Los Angeles International Airport (LAX) in 1949). Prior to that time, the main airport for Los Angeles was the Grand Central Airport in Glendale.

After years of destructive flooding and deaths, Ballona Creek would finally be channelized by the U.S. Army Corps of Engineers; lined with concrete and boulders barged the 26 mile route from Santa Catalina Island.

The Los Angeles Flood of 1938 was a major flooding event that was responsible for inundating much of Los Angeles, Orange, and Riverside counties, California, during early 1938. The flood was caused by a pair of oceanic storms that swept inland across the Los Angeles Basin in February and March 1938, causing abnormal rainfall across much of coastal Southern California. 113 to 115 people perished in the flood, which was one of the most catastrophic disasters in area history. For months, there was virtually no way to travel north from Westchester or Playa Del Rey, as the area below the Bluffs was almost completely underwater. At the intersection of Lincoln and Jefferson Boulevards, the water depth was close to 20 feet. This is a notable anomaly, as the area sits just 7 feet above sea level at those cross-streets.

Loyola University would celebrate it's tenth anniversary in 1939. On streets surrounding the college, homes were first erected for educators, and those homes remain as some of the oldest in the region. Still visible today in many of the sidewalks, including the sidewalk out side my own home, is the stamp; CLAUDE FISHER CO. CONTRACTOR 1929.

The streets surrounding the college ; the first neighborhood streets excavated in Westchester, were named for Jesuit colleges and schools; Fordham, Georgetown and Holy Cross to name a few. They are very narrow avenues, as the construction street gauge called for the width needed to accommodate a horse and buggy or a Ford Model-A. No one could have imagined the gargantuan SUV's of today. There is an urban legend that Julius Caesar specified a legal width for chariots at the width of *standard gauge*, causing road ruts at that width, so all later wagons had to have the same width or else risk having one set of wheels suddenly fall into one deep rut but not the other. Whatever the truth, 1920's construction was nonetheless affected by a multiple of standard gauge. Later streets were widened considerably.

To help lead students, educators and visitors to the college, palm trees were planted at Lincoln and 85th street, heading east down 85th Street past Campion and Gonzaga, and then heading north the full length of Loyola Boulevard, to the front gates of the university at 80th Street. 85th Street was paved; Manchester Boulevard was not.

In fact, as shown in early maps, Campion Avenue was not a street at all. It was a dirt path which ran the length of Lincoln Boulevard between Manchester and 83rd Street, and was called "Fordham Walk," referencing the place where the path merged with Fordham Road and the Loyola campus, at the then western edge of the university property. This "set-back" or easement and preservation of green space, was in common usage in early Westchester. From Sepulveda to Lincoln Boulevard for instance, the street we know today as 85th street; the east/west residential street north of Manchester Boulevard in Westchester, was a dirt path also.

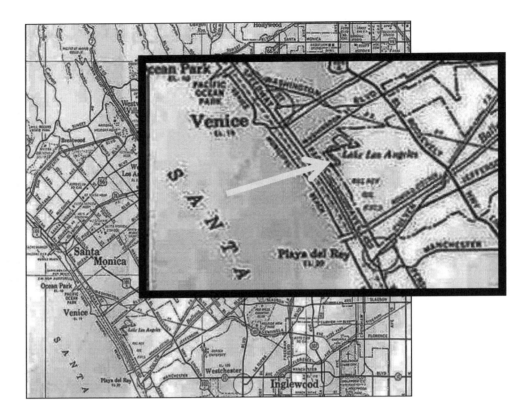

**LAKE LOS ANGELES.** The area below the Bluffs; Playa Del Rey, Westchester Playa Vista, and the Ballona Wetlands, is an ancient embayment that extended all the way to Baldwin Hills. It was the depository for the fresh water of Centinela and Walnut Creek's. Walnut Creek, which originated near the LA Coliseum at Exposition Boulevard, dried up sometime in the 1930's, when the City of Los Angeles developed an aggressive flood control plan for the region. At times, recorded in oral histories from the early 1800's through the 1950's, the current intersection of Lincoln and Jefferson Boulevards was only crossable by boat; and at times flooded for months at a time. The once natural, year round, spring-fed Centinela Creek; some of the purest drinking water in the region, would become the main drinking supply for the City of Inglewood. The remains of the creeks water would eventually be channelized, and then channeled underground near the intersection of Sepulveda and Centinela Boulevards, and finally directed into Ballona Creek. You can see the above ground concreted creek bed near the San Diego Freeway on-ramp, at the Howard Hughes Center. Centinela Creek provided the drinking and irrigation water for both Rancho La Ballona and Rancho Centinela Aguaje. After years of seasonal flooding, this map notes the area as Lake Los Angeles.(Complements, Google Books).

Campion Drive incidentally, was named for Campion Jesuit High School; a Jesuit-run boarding school for boys in Prairie du Chien, Wisconsin, named for the Jesuit martyr Edmund Campion.

In 1580, the Jesuit mission to England began. Campion accompanied Robert Persons who, as superior, was intended to counterbalance his own fervor and impetuousness, but he was arrested and accused of being a seditious Jesuit spy. Committed to the Tower of London, he was questioned in the presence of Queen Elizabeth, who asked him if he acknowledged her to be the true Queen of England. He replied in the affirmative, and she offered him wealth and dignities, but on condition of rejecting his Catholic faith, which he refused to accept. He was kept a long time in prison and reputedly racked twice. After spending his last days in prayer he was led with two companions to Tyburn and hanged, drawn and quartered on December 1, 1581, at the age of 41.

Campion Jesuit High School was founded in 1880, and from 1888-1898 the school was a private house of formation for Jesuit Novitiates and Philosophates. It is quite possible that one of the early Jesuits at Loyola had a hand in naming this street; it's origin unknown to most.

As they were excavated, the numbered streets in the area joined the existing street numbering grid of the city of Los Angeles, a practice not always followed below the Bluffs at Playa Del Rey, creating some tricky renaming and renumbering of streets in later days. And today's Culver Boulevard, which follows the Ballona Wetlands to the Village of Playa Del Rey, was at times called Speedway Boulevard and Del Rey Boulevard. Many years later, during the height of the Cold War frenzy, Moscow Street would be renamed a for a friendlier thing; a Sandpiper.

Finally, Waterloo Street, the street where Fritz Burns had erected his mansion, and where so to speak, *he had met his Waterloo,* would be renamed Waterview Street.

**SAINT VINCENT'S COLLEGE, 1875.** Now known as Loyola Marymount, University was located on Sixth and Broadway in downtown Los Angeles. (Complements, LAPL).

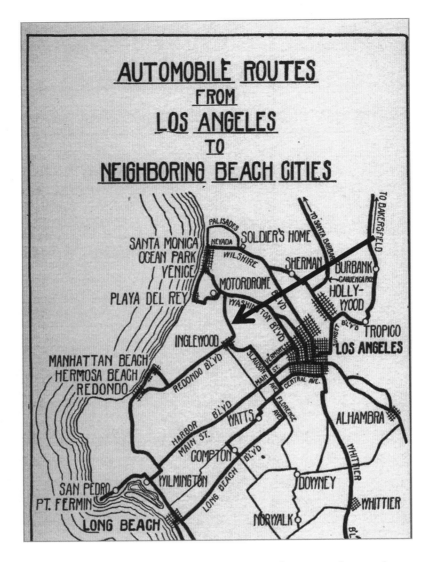

**1912 AAA AUTO MAP.** As of 1912, travel maps showed Inglewood's borders extending to the sea. (Complements, Los Angeles Public Library).

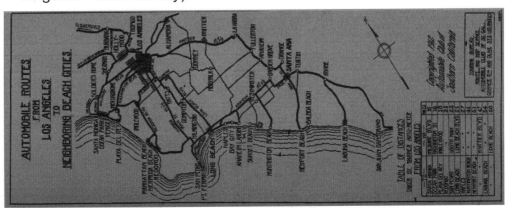

**UNDATED AAA MAP.** This 1920's era map begins to note changes in the Westchester area, and with the subdivision activities, separates Inglewood and Playa Del Rey from those newly developed areas. (Complements, Los Angeles Public Library).

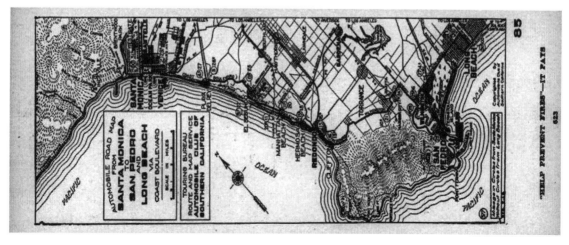

71

The Motordrome near Playa del Rey, Cal.

1910 BY A. B. DODGE, L. A.

**PLAYA DEL REY MOTORDOME, (sometimes called *Motordrome*), 1910.**
The first board track in the world opened at the Los Angeles Coliseum
Motordome at Playa del Rey, California, on April 8, 1910. Based on and utilizing
the same technology as the French velodromes used for bicycle races. The
track and others like it were created with thousands of 2 inch X 4 inch boards.
Air-shows were also held here. Note the un-channelized Ballona Creek in the
background, and the trolley tracks running alongside Speedway Boulevard in
the foreground. The lagoon extends half-way to Santa Monica. (Postcard,
Courtesy, Author).

# MOTOR AGE

VL. V. No. 1.     JANUARY 7, 1904.     $2.00 Per Year.

## A YEAR'S ACHIEVEMENT—A YEAR'S PROMISE

# WILL BE WORLD-FAMOUS FOR SPEED TESTS

**Where the Road Will Begin**

**Birdseye View of the Straightaway**

**Club Men Inspecting the Course**

Los Angeles, Cal., Jan. 4—What is destined to be the world's greatest automobile race course is being laid out near this city; on the plain between the southwest side of the city and the Pacific ocean. Where the course begins is about midway between this city and Santa Monica, near what is known as the Palms, a small village. As will be seen in illustrations, the starting point begins on the present highway at the end of a shaded strip of road bordered by full grown pepper trees, which almost meet over head.

The 7½ miles parallel the new short line, a double track trolley line which leaves the

California, were taken over the route with Superintendent Clark of the Los Angeles-Pacific Railway Co., and survey and estimates were thoroughly examined. Early in December the board of governors of the A. C. of S. C. considered carefully the proposition and voted to raise all the funds necessary to complete the straightaway in addition to the sum of $7,000 it already had set aside for this work.

The total cost of the 7½ miles will probably be about $30,000, and the boulevard will be fenced in, and closed at both ends substantially with gates, so that it can be closed

**1904, CHILTON'S MOTOR AGE; SPEEDWAY BOULEVARD (CULVER BOULEVARD) OPENS UP WESTSIDE TO THE AUTOMOBILE.** Views of the Auto Club sponsored "raceway." (Complements, Author; Chilton's Moor Age, January 7, 1904).

**FUND RAISER, 1928.** Loyola University's September 1928 dinner brought together more than 150 of the most influential figures in Los Angeles., to raise money for the construction of the Westchester campus.

Back row, left to right: John A. Van Kuik, William Bearman, Fritz B. Burns, Frank M. Flynn, Edward C. Purpus, Frank Muller, Harry Langdon and James J. Donahue. Middle row, left to right: Father W.E. Corr, Winfield Sheehan, Joseph Scott, Isidore B. Dockweiler, John G. Mott, Supervisor John H. Bean, Rev. Edwin P. Ryland, R.F. Del Valle and Judge Benjamin F. Bledsoe. Front row, left to right: Samuel T. Clover, E.P. Clark, Loyola University President Joseph A. Sullivan, S.J., Louis B. Mayer, Judge Louis W. Myers, George W. Eastman, George I. Cochran, Harry F. Chandler and John G. Bullock. (Complements, Wikipedia).

**LOYOLA UNIVERSITY LOS ANGELES, 1928.** Scale model of the future campus of Loyola University of Los Angeles is displayed in front of the William H. Evans real estate agency as a sales promotion for homes and businesses in "California's new cultural district." (Complements, Google Books).

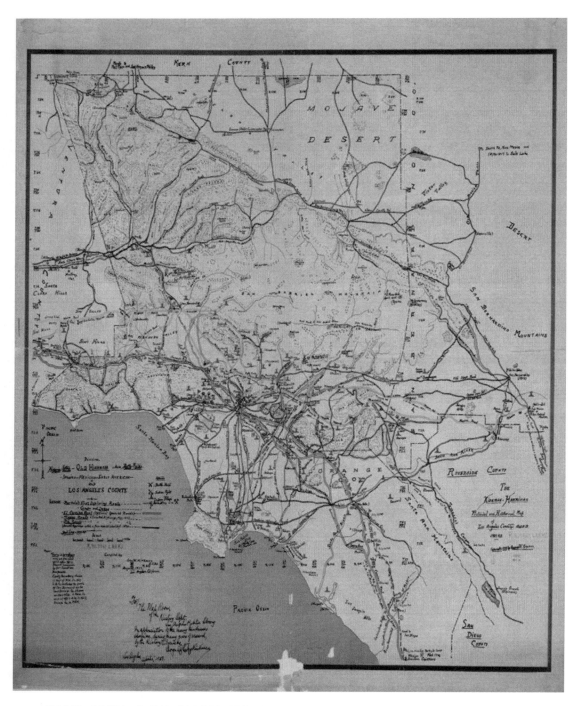

**MAP, 1937, LOS ANGELES.** Kirkman-Harriman Pictorial and
Historical Map of Los Angeles County 1860-1937, creator: George W.
Kirkman. (Courtesy, LAPL).

**EL SEGUNDO FARM, 1911, PAY-DAY, STANDARD REFINERY, 1912.** Daniel Freeman sold portions of the rancho to multiple owners. George H. Peck (1856–1940) owned the 840 acres (3.4 km$^2$) of land the Chevron Refinery now sits on. Peck also developed land in neighboring El Porto where a street still stands to his name. The city earned its name because it was the site of the second ("el segundo" in Spanish) Standard Oil refinery on the West Coast when Standard Oil purchased the 840 acres, of farm land in 1911. This is now known as the Chevron Refinery. The city was incorporated in 1917. (Complements, Wikipedia).

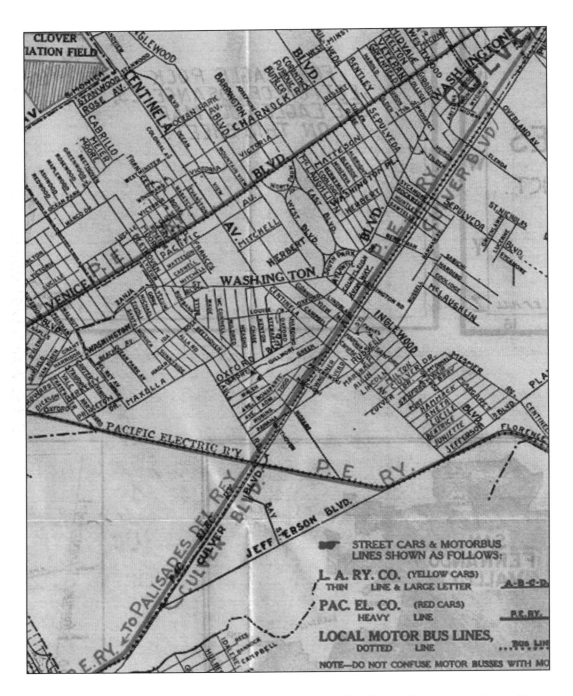

**1924, REGIONAL TRANSPORTATION MAP.** In the lower/center/left of the map, the Los Angeles Pacific Electric Railway tracks, cross the Ballona Wetlands. (Complements, Author).

**PIONEER BAKERY, VENICE, CA.** Just across Ballona Creek, from a Venice storefront in 1908, Jean Baptise Garacochea used sourdough starters he brought with him from the Basque country, and the Pioneer Bakery grew from a small neighborhood-serving enterprise, to a line of sourdough breads, The enterprise was originally called the National French Bakery. French rolls and specialties, were distributed throughout the Westchester/ Playa Del Rey region and all over Southern California. The full scale bakery, which made artisan breads long before it was fashionable, eventually moved to Rose Avenue in 1917. It was not until the early 1940's that a scratch-bakery opened in Westchester, on Sepulveda Boulevard. (Courtesy, Google Books).

**EL SEGUNDO, 1911.** Standard Oil started cleaning up land for its refinery. Photo taken just before construction was started. (Courtesy, LAPL).

**THE DEAL RESTAURANT, EL SEGUNDO, 1914.** It was one of the few structures on the Richmond Street business block which was destroyed by fire on May 10, 1917. In 1914, El Segundo's population was only 1,200. (Courtesy, LAPL).

**EL SEGUNDO RESTAURANT; STREET CORNER, 1915.** Next door is the R.A. Johnson Drug Co., and T.J. Divine dry Goods and groceries. El Segundo was so named because it followed El Primera; Richmond, CA, on San Francisco Bay, Standard Oil's first large refinery location. (Courtesy, LAPL).

**1914 EL SEGUNDO CELEBRATION.** Residents of El Segundo gathered for celebration of the coming of the first Pacific Electric car, on direct line from Los Angeles, in 1914. The Pacific Electric helped the growth of El Segundo. (Courtesy, LAPL).

**PLAYA DEL REY LAGOON, 1902.** Beginning in 1902, the Beach Land Company began buying up acreage at Ballona Harbor, and building a grand resort. In the end, they purchased one thousand acres of land, including the lagoon and two and one half miles of beach frontage. Worcester, Massachusetts born Henry Parkhurst Barbour was the President of the Beach Land Company and in 1888-90, one of principal promoters Gray's Harbor Country, WA. He would go on to develop the Long Beach, California Harbor in 1905. Barbour died of a massive brain hemorrhage in 1911. Like Gillis, Trask, and Rindge, (other stockholders), a street in Playa Del Rey was named for him. (Courtesy, Los Angeles Public Library).

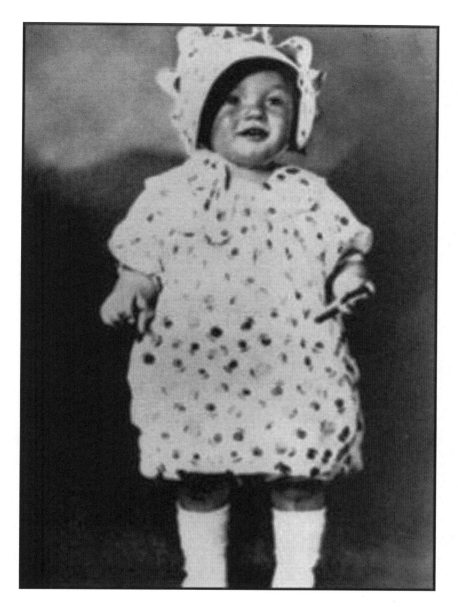

**NEARBY; IN HAWTHORNE, CA, 1927.** From 1926 to 1932, this young lady lived at 459 East Rhode Island Street (134th), in Hawthorne. She attended Ballona Elementary Kindergarten from 1931-1932 at age 5-6. Later in life, she would often travel back to the former Rancho Sausal Redondo; flying in and out of Los Angeles International Airport at Westchester, CA. The answer to who she is, can be found on page 220. (Complements, Google).

**LOYOLA UNIVERSITY LOS ANGELES, GROUNDBREAKING, DEDICATION, AND GRADUATION CEREMONY, 1928.** Founded in 1911, Loyola Marymount University (LMU) is a co-educational private Roman Catholic Jesuit university located at 1 LMU Drive, in the Westchester area of Los Angeles. The present University is the successor to the pioneer Catholic college and first institution of higher learning in Southern California. In 1865, the Vincentian Fathers inaugurated St. Vincent's College for boys in Los Angeles, originally located in the Lugo Adobe House. Rapid growth prompted the Jesuits to seek a new campus in 1917 on Venice Boulevard and was incorporated as Loyola College of Los Angeles in 1918. In 1929, it relocated once again, this time to its present Westchester campus, and the school achieved university status one year later, becoming Loyola University of Los Angeles. Dedication services were held at the future site of Loyola University, in the Westchester area of Los Angeles. A long line of men dressed in academic gowns appear to be walking in a row. Massive crowds attended the historic dedication, as visible by this photograph. (Courtesy, LAPL).

**LOYOLA GROUNDBREAKING, 1928.** LMU sits atop a bluff of 150 acres in the Del Rey Hills of West Los Angeles. The original 99 acres were donated to the university by Harry Culver. Xavier Hall, named for St. Francis Xavier, S.J., a companion of St. Ignatius of Loyola, S.J., and St. Robert's Hall, named for St. Robert Bellarmine, S.J., a cardinal and Doctor of the Church, were the first two buildings to be built on the current Westchester Campus. Following their completion in 1929, Xavier Hall housed both the Jesuit Faculty and the students at the time while St. Robert's Hall served as the academic and administrative building. (Complements, LAPL).

**1928 COMMENCEMENT.** Men in academic gowns sit shoulder-to-shoulder at the dedication services of Loyola University's future home. Father Joseph Sullivan sits in front row. (Complements, LAPL).

**LOYOLA GROUNDBREAKING, 1928.** The College operates its own newspaper; The *Los Angeles Loyolan*. The newspaper has been published for over 80 years. It was originally titled *"The Cinder"* for the cinders kicked up by the trains passing the downtown campus of St. Vincent's College. (Complements, LAPL).

**LOYOLA GROUNDBREAKING, 1928.** Harry H. Culver, (in suit) and his wife with Father Joseph Sullivan, at the first Loyola University of Los Angeles commencement. It was held at the Westchester Campus before the buildings were erected. Culver donated 100 acres of land to the university which, in return, awarded him an honorary degree. (Complements, LAPL).

**NATIONAL AIR RACES, WESTCHESTER, CA, 1928.** The US soldiers surrounding the plane are U.S. Army. The United States Army Air Corps (USAAC) was a forerunner of the United States Air Force. Created on July 2, 1926 as part of the United States Army, it was also the predecessor of the United States Army Air Forces (USAAF), established in 1941. Although abolished as an organization in 1942, the Air Corps (AC) remained as a branch of the Army until 1947. Below, an air race usher. (Complements, LAPL).

**NATIONAL AIR RACES, WESTCHESTER, CA, 1928**. An Army PT-1 plane powered by a Hisso engine at Mines Field (Los Angeles International Airport) in Westchester during the 1928 National Air Races. Developed from the Dayton-Wright TW-3 airplane, the PT-1, used by the Army for training purposes, featured a welded fuselage framework of chrome-molybdenum steel tubing, which proved so sturdy and dependable that the plane earned the nickname "Trusty." This air competition, comprised of a series of pylon and cross-country races, took place annually from 1920 to 1949. Due to the rapid development of aviation science during those years, there was significant popular interest in this event. Army Air Corp size; 14,650 men, 1,646 aircraft (1932), 16,863 men, 855 aircraft (1936), 152,125 men, 6,777 aircraft (1941). (Complements, LAPL).

**DEL REY HILLS, DEL REY LAGOON, 1924.** The vast expanse in the upper areas of the photograph would later became parts of Playa Del Rey, Westchester and LAX. (Courtesy, Los Angeles Public Library).

**MINES FIELD (LAX), 1931.** (Complements, Wikipedia).

**NATIONAL AIR RACES, WESTCHESTER, CA, 1928**. Men examine a Travel Air plane powered by a Wright J-5 engine at Mines Field (later became the Los Angeles International Airport) in Westchester during the 1928 National Air Races. Developed from the Dayton-Wright TW-3 airplane, the PT-1, used by the Army for training purposes, featured a welded fuselage framework of chrome-molybdenum steel tubing, which proved so sturdy and dependable that the plane earned the nickname "Trusty." This air competition, comprised of a series of pylon and cross-country races, took place annually from 1920 to 1949. Due to the rapid development of aviation science during those years, there was significant popular interest in this event. The 1928 races ran from September 8-16. (Complements, LAPL).

**NATIONAL AIR RACES, WESTCHESTER, CA, 1928.** Famous cowgirl Vera McGinnis (1895-1990) in aviation attire pushes a plow-like implement at Mines Field (Los Angeles International Airport) in Westchester during the 1928 National Air Races as a crowd watches on. The "plow" is used to help make the planes come to a complete stop on the ground. This air competition, comprised of a series of pylon and cross-country races, took place annually from 1920 to 1949. (Complements, LAPL).

**1932 LOS ANGELES OLYMPIAD.** Los Angeles, California hosted the 1932 Olympics. Organizing and operating the equestrian events was the task of the Army, in particular the cavalry. The cross-county eventing was held at Westchester, CA. The Great Depression of the 1930's was at its height in 1932 and this limited the number of equestrian teams able to travel to the US. For the US team however, this was their Olympics and with the mentorship of General Henry they prepared for the 1932 Olympics as they had for no other games. The results reflected this effort. The jumping team, led by Major Harry Chamberlin riding Show Girl in his fourth Olympics, won a Silver Medal in jumping. Lieutenant Earl "Tommy" Thomson on Jenny Camp led the eventing team. Lieutenant Thomson earned an individual Silver Medal and the team turned in a Gold Medal performance: the first US equestrian gold. Even more brilliant was the effort of Captain Hiram Tuttle, who, as a Quartermaster officer, was one of the few officers who was not either a cavalryman or artilleryman. He rode his own horse, Olympic, to a Bronze Medal in dressage as part of the US dressage team that also won the team Bronze Medal. The games ended with the US earning five medals. This feat was unmatched for over fifty years until the USET team earned five medals at the 1984 Los Angeles games. The '32 Olympic games, although limited in the scope of participants, demonstrated that the US Cavalry was back as a force in international equestrian competition, and foretold great things for the 1936 Olympics in Berlin. (Complements, LAPL).

**THE OLYMPICS AT WESTCHESTER, 1932.** Lieutenant Tommy Thomson on *Jenny Camp;* finishing the Cross Country Course en route to a Silver Individual and Gold Team Medal. (Complements, USET).

**HARRY CHAMBERLAIN, ABOARD PLEASANT SMILES.** Major Harry Chamberlin was the Team Captain at the 1932 Olympic Games. He rode in both the show jumping, and the Three Day Event. His mount for the Three Day competition was an off-the-track bay Thoroughbred, *Pleasant Smiles.* The two turned a very solid performance marred only by a fall over a tricky jump on the cross country. The fall caused them to finish in 4th place individually. (Complements , *Rider Magazine*).

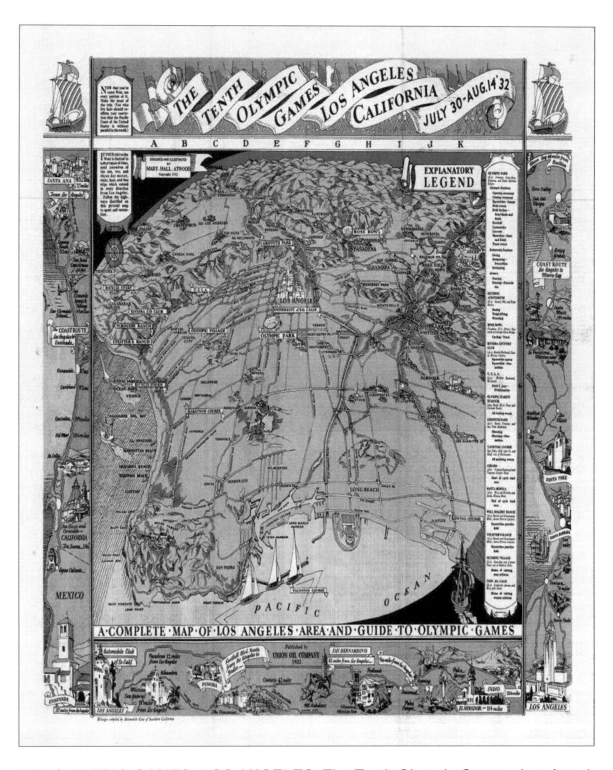

**1932 OLYMIPIC GAMES, LOS ANGELES.** The Tenth Olympic Games, Los Angeles, California, creator: Mary Hall-Atwood. (Courtesy, LAPL).

**HOME DELIVERY; HELM'S BAKERY TRUCK, WESTCHESTER, 1955.**
Since it's early years, the Helms Bakery used Divco Twin coaches to deliver
their baked goods. The Helms Bakery Divco fleet was one of the largest in the
United States. In later years, they supplemented their fleet with Chevrolet
panel trucks. The Helms Bakery was located on Venice Boulevard (inset). The
Bakery had a strong sports heritage. Their Olympic Bread commemorated
their official sponsorship of the 1932 Olympics, which were held in Los
Angeles. In 1936 they founded the Helms Athletic Hall of Fame. This became
a model for the many sports halls of fame existing today. Olympic Bread was
also said to nourish our Apollo 11 astronauts on their way to the moon! At one
point four routes covered Westchester. Many dairies also serviced the area,
and along with many milkmen, after 38 years of delivering the very finest in
baked goods, the Helmsman stopped coming in 1969.(Courtesy, Frank J.
Leskovitz). Also inset, 1940's British made Acme Helm's Bakery 2-tone whistle.
(Authors collection).

**WESTSIDE INTERURBAN SERVICE, 1920's and 1930's; FLORENCE AVENUE.**
The *5 line* was the longest line on *LARY,* running from Townsend and Colorado in Eagle Rock to Broadway and Hawthorne Blvd . in Hawthorne. The line had many miles of private right of way. In the 1920s the line was designated the "E" because it ran along Eagle Rock Boulevard. The comprehensive transit plan of the 1920s proposed to elevate this line onto embankment and viaduct from Grand and Figueroa to Inglewood and patch it into a proposed downtown subway. The portion of this line from Grand and Jefferson to Hawthorne was built originally by the Los Angeles and Redondo Railway in 1902, and was originally on private right of way the entire length. The photo below is a rush hour shot showing three outbound *5 line* streetcars running on the private right of way along  Florence Avenue. (Courtesy, uncanny. net).

**MINES FIELD, 1934.** Airport officials, at the former Bennet Brothers Rancho, used some ingenious methods to keep the grass trimmed. Local ranchers were invited to graze their sheep on the runways. (Courtesy, Huntington Library).

**MINES FIELD.** The runway at Mines Field (later to become the Los Angeles International Airport). (Courtesy, LAPL).

**MINES FIELD, 1930.** Aerial view of Mines Field and surroundings; Inglewood and Hawthorne, CA. The tree lined street intersecting the photo is Aviation Boulevard. Mines Field later to become the Los Angeles International Airport. (Complements, LAPL).

**NATIONAL AIR RACES, 1928.** Fliers seeking Mines Field, new municipal airport and site of the National Air Races, will hereafter find the way pointed out to them unmistakably by six huge aerial markers. All over Southern California, on barn roofs and in fields, these markers showed them the way to Westchester. (Complements, LAPL).

**AVIATION BOULEVARD.** Rushing work to make the Los Angeles Municipal Airport the safest landing place in the country, workmen are shown felling huge trees that line the eastern boundary of the field. Col. Richard B. Barnitz, Director of the Airport, and L. G. Holonbeck of the United States Bureau of Air Commerce are shown inspecting the removal of the trees. (Courtesy, LAPL).

**MINES FIELD RACEWAY, WESTCHESTER, 1934.** The massive race course and grounds, backed by oil magnate Earl Gilmore, covered a territory from Century Boulevard to the south; and north to Arbor Vitae/Will Rogers; and between Sepulveda Blvd. and Inglewood Ave. The location had previously played host to the National Air Races and Aeronautical Exposition in 1928, and was visited by the Graf Zeppelin, and flying pioneer Charles Lindberg. To attend the Air Races, Amelia Earhart completed the west-bound leg of the first woman's solo, U.S. transcontinental round trip; landing at Los Angeles. This 2 mile dirt course (it was never paved) drew crowds from everywhere, and the grand stands alone held 75,000 people. Local favorites such as Rex Mays, Kelly Petillo and Lou Moore raced here. The whole enterprise lasted only 4 years, 1932 to 1936; but hundreds of thousands of spectators flocked there. (Complements, Author).

**BALLONA CREEK, UNCHANNELED, 1920's**. View of the Creek where it passes through present day Playa Vista, and into the Ballona Wetlands. (Complements, Doug Linnett).

**1934, MINES FIELD, EDDIE MEYER.** The second race of the Gilmore Gold Cup series was run at a B-shaped course on property leased from the city of Los Angeles in February of 1934. The first race at Mines Field drew a crowd said to be bigger than those at the popular air races and was estimated at 75,000 by the Times.  Even if that estimate carried some hot air, plenty of fans lined the fences of the long front straight of the two-mile track, many in their own vehicles as well as in the grandstands. Given that the field was made up of "blue bloods" of racing, including Indy 500 winners Louis Meyer and Pete De Paulo as well as future Indy winner Wilbur Shaw plus local heroes Rex Mays and Kelly Petillo, the Indy winner in 1935, the Mines Field race had high a very high profile. Eddie Rickenbacker, the famed World War I flying ace and chairman of the AAA Contest Board, was among a long list of dignitaries to attend the event. (Complements, racintoday.com).

**THE LOS ANGELES HYPERION WORKS, PLAYA DEL REY, CA, 1925.**
Opened in the late 1800's, and located on the bluffs above the beach at
Imperial Highway and Vista Del Mar, the city installed a "screening system"
in 1925. Prior to that time, and since 1894, raw/untreated sewage was
dumped directly into the Santa Monica Bay through an offshore pipe, called
an outfall, outraging local swimmers. In 1888, a prominent figure, Juan
Carillo canvassed the La Ballona residents, now Playa Del Rey and Playa
Vista, and succeeded in stopping the construction of a second outfall at
Pier Avenue and Venice Boulevard. Today, the Los Angeles Hyperion has
installed many new technologically driven systems to prevent raw sewage
entering into Santa Monica Bay at Dockweiler State Beach. (Complements,
Los Angeles Public Library).

**1930's STREET CAR, CRENSHAW AND MANCHESTER BOULEVARDS.** (Complements, LAPL).

**MINES FIELD,1939.** Aerial view of Mines Field, now Los Angeles Municipal Airport. The field was sold to Los Angeles by William W. Mines. It was the former Bennet Brothers Ranch.(Complements, LAPL).

**COACH TOM LIEB, WITH IGGY THE LION, 1935.** Football coach Tom Lieb poses for a photograph with Lions mascot Lil' Akron. The Loyola University of Los Angeles' football team, the Lions, competed as an independent against teams from the Pacific Coast Conference and the Pacific Coast Intercollegiate Conference from 1921 to 1951. Tom Lieb, Knute Rockne's assistant came to coach Loyola football after the Notre Dame coach turned down the offer to move to California. Here is Tom Lieb with lion mascot Lil' Akron, a gift from the Associated Students of the University of Arizona. (Complements, LAPL). Although its origin is somewhat clouded, the Lion mascot, known as Iggy the Lion after St. Ignatius of Loyola, S.J., has been synonymous with Loyola Marymount University for more than 70 years. During the 1930s, 1940s, and 1950s Loyola University shared its mascot Metro-Goldwyn-Mayer (MGM). The MGM Lion was brought to campus on the days of athletic events and university ceremonies to serve as the official school mascot (Leo the Lion was the first in the 1930s). Today, student rumors hold that the lion would stay overnight in Xavier Hall and others hold that the lion's permanent home was on the campus' bluff between Xavier Hall and Sacred Heart Chapel. Louis B. Mayer had been a major contributor to the university when the school first moved to the Del Rey Hills and began building its first buildings. Inset, 1933 Football Program, vs. Nevada; 10-13-1933. (Complements, Authors Collection).

**TOM LIEB'S FIGHTING LIONS, 1936.** (Complements, John Wilson, San Pedro, CA, LMU '73). ). Inset, 1933 Football Program, vs. USC.(Complements, Authors Collection).

**MARCHING BAND.** The Loyola Marching Band, Gilmore Stadium, 1935. The Loyola .Band was a major attraction for years at Gilmore Stadium, the Los Angeles Coliseum, and the Pasadena Rose Bowl. (Complements, LAPL).

***ON THE ROAD* AT LOYOLA, 1930's.** Bob Hope and Bing Crosby on the Loyola Links practice golf course, with Father Lorenzo Malone. Bob Hope was a major donor to Loyola University and Bing Crosby was a great benefactor of Gonzaga University in Spokane. The land formerly occupied by the Loyola Links practice golf course later became the site of the Burns Fine Arts Center and the Von der Ahe Communication Arts Building. Arguably, this was the first golf course in Westchester. (Complements, LAPL).

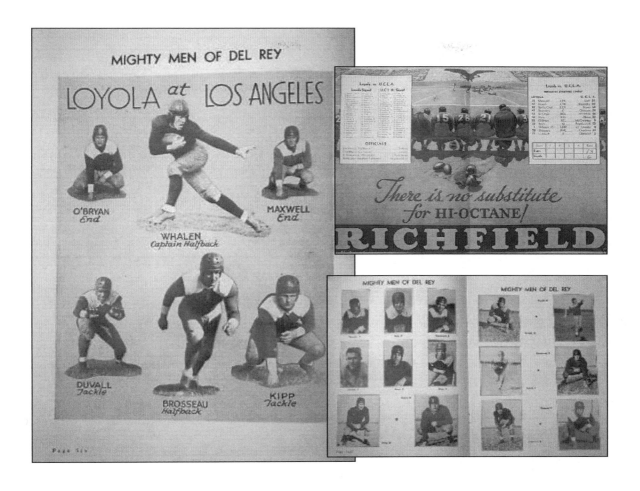

**LOYOLA LIONS vs. UCLA BRUINS, 1934**. *The Mighty Men of Del Rey*; the 1934 Loyola Lion Football squad. Westchester had not been named yet, and most folks referred to the Jesuit campus as Playa Del Rey, Venice or just "Loyola". Coached by ex-Notre Dame Assistant and Line Coach, Tom Lieb, Loyola fielded an impressive squad throughout the 1930's. Playing UCLA in 1934, Coach Lieb was very familiar with his opponent. The Bruins were coached by Bill Spaulding, who Lieb had competed against while coaching Notre Dame, and Spaulding at Kalamazoo, and later while at Wisconsin, while Spaulding was coaching Minnesota. Loyola also competed against UCLA in baseball, track and hockey. Lieb also coached the Loyola Lion Hockey Team. Many of the Loyola Football games were played at Gilmore Stadium near Fairfax, Cursen Street and Beverly Boulevard. That year, another Los Angeles landmark opened close by, the Original Farmers Market. (Complements, examiner. com).

**LOYOLA CAMPUS, WESTCHESTER.** The administrative building of Loyola University of Los Angeles , on June 2, 1937. (Courtesy, LAPL).

**LOYOLA FOOTBALL, 1935.** The Loyola University football team engaging in comic publicity on their practice field near Loyola Blvd. and 80th Street. The players pose with marching band instruments in front of a goalpost. (Complements, LAPL). Inset, ticket. Loyola vs. St. Mary's. L.A. Coliseum, 101-5-1939. (Complements, Authors Collection).

**LOYOLA BASKETBALL.** The 1938 Loyola Lions, clockwise from top: Coach Needles, Kanne, Newell, Havaland, McDonald, Rocovich, Quigley, Kriste, Sweeters, Palamatary, Schneiders, McGarry and Woolpert. (Complements, 1938 Lair Annual, published by the students of Loyola University of Los Angeles; provided by Dr. Joseph P. Callinan, Loyola University, Class of '56).

**LOYOLA CAMPUS, WESTCHESTER, 1937.** The school fielded many dominant sporting teams since 1906, when LU then known as St. Vincent's College, started a basketball team. The initial season of LMU athletics offered a glimpse of things to come as the Lions posted a 5-0 record in that first season. (Although, prior to 1906 St. Vincent's fielded football and baseball teams that played YMCA and other similar teams). (Complements, LAPL).

**WILL ROGERS STREET AND WILEY POST AVENUE.** Will Rogers, named after the cowboy humorist (above left), is located just north of public parking lot C near Los Angeles International Airport (LAX). Will Rogers Street branches northeast between Westchester Parkway and Manchester Avenue where it is renamed Wiley Post Avenue, after Will Rogers' friend and pilot, who was also killed in the plane crash which took Rogers' life in 1935. Post (above right) was the first pilot to fly solo around the world. Photo below, (that's Will Rogers in the hat and tie, standing on the wing) was taken on August 15, 1935 shortly before taking off from a lagoon near Point Barrow Alaska. (Complements, *Wikipedia*).

**NEAR THE CORNER OF MANCHESTER BOULEVARD AND PERSHING DRIVE, 1931.** (Courtesy, A.B. Brad Fowler Collection).

# Four
## THE WAR, THE AIRPORT AND A KID FROM TEXAS

Building a town or city is about infrastructure first, and Westchester in many respects perfected its infrastructure over time. Wide roads leading to the town, the beginnings of a vibrant shopping center, utilities and power sources were erected all through the area. The town boasted a superior college university and easy access to some of the best beaches in the world. A fire station was opened, and all of this was close to a state-of-the-art hospital; Daniel Freeman Memorial, which although planned in the 1940's, would open in the next decade.

As the Nation, and moreover the world prepared for war new housing starts continued around the town at a steady pace.

If Daniel Freeman is called the Father of Inglewood, then it is hard to imagine calling anyone but Fritz Bernard Burns, Father of Westchester.

Fully recovered from his devastating 1920's losses, Burns began developments all over Southern California, including Westchester and Playa Del Rey.

Also in 1940, a young industrialist; *the Kid from Texas*; Howard Hughes, moved to Westchester.

Howard Hughes established a new aircraft division within his Hughes Tool Company in 1932. The first facilities of the new aircraft division were in space rented from the Lockheed Company in Burbank. By 1939 the Hughes Tool Company was engaged in a full-scale program to develop a high speed fighter bomber using Duramold plywood, a plastic-bonded plywood molded under heat & high pressure. This became the DX-2, later known simply as the D-2. To build the D-2, the Burbank facility would be insufficient, and Hughes sought a much larger facility.

In 1940 Hughes purchased 380 acres (although other sources put the initial purchase as over 1,000 acres) of the Ballona Wetlands just west of Culver City for $500,000.

Hughes recognized the area as one of the few large tracts of remaining undeveloped land in Los Angeles. The high water table made it necessary to sink 50' pilings into the wetlands to support Hughes' buildings & reroute the course of the Centinela River, which flowed through the site every spring and flooded it.

On his new land Hughes constructed a 60,000 square foot air conditioned, humidity-controlled aircraft plant with an adjacent grass runway. The earliest depiction of the Hughes Airport which has been located, was on a 1940 Los Angeles street map.

By the weekend of the July 4th, 1941, all of the operations of Hughes Aircraft were relocated from Burbank to the new Culver City Plant. The Hughes Culver City plant had an initial workforce of just 250 employees (later to grow into the thousands). The D-2 was built in secret at the Hughes Culver City factory with longtime Hughes associate, Glenn Odekirk, providing engineering inputs.

The fighter that emerged from the Hughes experimental shop looked like a scaled-up P-38 Lightning and on paper, sported similar performance potential. The D-2 had a twin-boom configuration, powered by a pair of 2,000 hp Pratt & Whitney R-2800s.

**HOWARD HUGHES, 1942.** This is the earliest photo which has been located of the Hughes Westchester plant . Hughes is inspecting the prototype of the Hughes D-2. (Complements, LAPL).

When the D-2 prototype was ready for final assembly in May 1943, it was relocated to Hughes' secretive facility at Harper Dry Lake in the Mojave Desert, from where it also conducted its flights.

In 1943, Hughes built the world's longest private runway in the world at Westchester. Runway 5/23 was 9,600' long - nearly 2 miles in length. It was not paved for its first few years, because Hughes believed that paved runways imparted unnecessary stress on an aircraft's landing gear. He reportedly had to add fill regularly to keep the ground solid.

Building 15, (also known as the Hughes Cargo Building) was built in 1943. It was the Hughes plant's signature structure. It was a giant double-gabled hangar, measuring 742' x 248', with Hughes' name painted on the roof.

One of the most famous projects to come out of the Hughes Culver City facility was the HK-1 Hercules flying boat, (better known as the "Spruce Goose").

As WW2 continued to rage, with the supply of strategic metals becoming constrained. Hughes became convinced that wood would be a logical substitute to replace metal in the construction of aircraft. He formed a joint venture with Henry Kaiser to develop a flying boat, which could serve as an "air bridge", linking the US with overseas allies & bypassing the U-boats which threatened shipping traffic. The aircraft which was developed, the HK-1 Hercules, was the largest airplane ever built (and continues to have the largest wingspan of any aircraft to the present day), its entire airframe was made of laminated wood.

The HK-1 was built in the giant Building 15 (also known as the Hughes Cargo Building). As large as the Cargo Building was, it wasn't quite big enough to house the gigantic plane. The hull & wings were built as separate units & sent off to Long Beach for assembly.

Unfortunately, the Hercules project did not result in any production, as WW2 ended before the aircraft was ready & the government did not see fit to order any examples. The sole prototype of the HK-1 spent the next 38 years in storage in a specially-constructed climate-controlled hangar in Long Beach.

On December 7th, 1941 Japanese Imperial Forces bombed Pearl Harbor, Hawaii. The contributions to the war effort by Westchester companies and residents was almost immeasurable.

Perhaps no other local company contributed to the war effort more than North American Aviation. It is often mentioned that North American was an Inglewood company, but in fact it was based in Westchester, and controlled by General Motors.

North American Aviation contributed three great aircraft to the Allied cause during World War II: the "AT-6 Texan" trainer, the "P-51 Mustang" fighter, and the "B-25 Mitchell" medium bomber.

While the Mustang is clearly the most famous of the three, the Mitchell was likely the most important aircraft in its own class, built in large quantity and proving its worth in both the Pacific and European theaters of war. In particular, the Mitchell gave America one of its first victories during the dark days of early 1942, when Jimmy Doolittle's raiders swept over Japan to humiliate the enemy.

In the years leading up to World War II, the North American Aviation (NAA) company led by President James H. "Dutch" Kindelberger, developed new aircraft to help meet the demands of the US military in preparation for war. In 1936, in response to a US Army Air Corps (USAAC) competition for a new medium bomber, NAA developed a twin-engine "tail dragger" aircraft designated the "NA-21", with the aircraft's first flight on 22 December 1936.

North American will also be remembered in history as one of the few companies in history ever taken over by the United States Army, under Executive Order from President Franklin D. Roosevelt.

NORTH AMERICAN B-25J MITCHELL (GVG / PD)

Unhappy over wage concessions, this conflict came to a head with the Roosevelt administration's use of military power to crush a strike, when a walkout by 4,000 workers in June of 1941 at the North American Aviation plant occurred.

This was the largest strike in California since the maritime general strike of 1934. A period of shop floor organizing and worker/employer polarization was brought to a head when the night shift suddenly walked off the job. Even the Communist-leaning officers of the local were caught by surprise. The workers did not resort to a sit down strike because such actions had just been declared illegal by the Supreme Court; instead, they organized a mass picket line that surrounded the plant.

UAW leader Dick Frankensteen had previously told the workers that they shouldn't worry about strike authorization since "it's just a scrap of paper anyway." However, the unauthorized nature of the work stoppage, and the visible presence of local Communists, were seen by the Roosevelt administration as providing a convenient opportunity for a show of force to discourage strikes in war industries.

Under pressure from the Roosevelt Administration, Frankensteen tried to order the strikers back to work at a meeting outside the plant, but was shouted down. He then put the local union under the control of an appointed administrator. Though he knew low wages, not "Communist agitation," was responsible for the strike, Frankensteen denounced local Communist activists in a national radio broadcast -- a virtual invitation to government intervention.

With the approval of top CIO leaders, troops broke up the mass picket lines around the plant and imposed virtual martial law in the immediate area. In smashing the strike with troops, and threatening strikers with induction into the army, FDR sent a strong message to the CIO leaders that their organizations were at risk if they allowed disruption of his program for imperialist war. The upshot was soon apparent as the CIO leaders capitulated to FDR's demands for a total "no strike" pledge when the U.S. finally entered the world war.

After the war, North American would go on to build the F-86 Sabre jet fighter, and the X-15 rocket plane, as well as Apollo Command and Service Module, the second stage of the Saturn V rocket, the Space Shuttle orbiter and the B-1 Lancer. Through a series of mergers and sales, North American Aviation is now part of Boeing.

As I said earlier, as the town of Westchester grew, the numbered streets followed the numbering grid of Los Angeles. But is some areas, they were named to remind us of the rich history of aviation, and the men, women and machines, who helped to create that history.

The streets of Kittyhawk, Will Rogers, Wiley Post, DeHaviland, Bleriot, Jenny, Glider, Liberator and Interceptor, Earhart, and Lilienthal; to name a few, all remind us of the aircraft history of the town.

As the Second World War ended, the new homes of Westchester couldn't be built fast enough. Back at Loyola University, which had served as a officer training program for both Army and Navy officers, then university President Father Edward Whelan, S.J., recognized the grave injustice of the Japanese internment camps during World War II and hired and housed many Japanese Americans returning to Los Angeles after their return from the camps.

In 1949, Father Charles Cassassa, S.J., Ph.D., was named president and began one of the most consequential presidencies in the university's history. His work included the formation of a graduate division on the Westchester campus occurred in June 1950, although the graduate work had formed an integral part of the Teacher Education Program during the preceding two years, expanding campus infrastructure, and started the Institute of Human Relations to promote improved racial relations in business and in government. Future Mayor of Los Angeles, Tom Bradley attended the first year-long program held by the Institute of Human Relations and remained life long friends with Father Cassassa.

Father Cassassa also continued Father Whelan's legacy of combating racial injustice. In 1950, he forced the school's football team to forfeit a game an away game against Texas Western since the school's rules prevented African-American players, such as Loyola's Bill English, to play on their field

**FRITZ B. BURNS, 1899-1979.** This is a later studio portrait of Burns; former president of the National Association of House Builders. Photo dated: August 27, 1953. Federal incentives for the private construction of housing, for employees in defense production facilities during World War II and for returning veterans immediately following the War, fostered dramatic changes in home building practices. Builders began to apply the principles of mass production, standardization, and pre-fabrication to house construction on a large scale. Builders like Fritz B. Burns and Fred W. Marlow of California began to build communities of an unprecedented size, such as Westchester in southeast Los Angeles, where more than 2,300 homes were built to FHA standards between 1941 and 1944. A copy of this photo hangs on the wall above the authors workspace. (Complements, LAPL).

**PLAYA DEL REY AT WAR, 1944.** On the sand dunes above Vista Del Mar at Imperial Highway, just across the street from the Los Angeles Hyperion Plant, three tactical batteries and coastal gun emplacements were established as part of the Harbor Defense Plan. After World War II, the guns were partially dismantled and buried in the dunes, where they remain to this day. On 14 December, Battery D, 144th FA, reported for duty and was assigned positions at Santa Monica and Playa del Rey. Sinister reports came in on 28 December. An unidentified submarine was reported off the Standard Oil wharf at Estero Bay at 1720 hours. The Navy tanker "RAMAPO" reported being followed by a surface craft approximately 450 miles southwest of Guadalupe. San Diego Naval Air Station sent out two planes to attack the pursuing vessel. The results of the attack were not given, but the vessel subsequently was identified as the Japanese Seaplane Tender: "KUNIKAWA MARU". This was denied by the Japanese Navy. Batteries D and F, 144th FA were concentrated at Redondo Beach and Playa del Rey. (Photos: Courtesy, Google Books).

**STAFF SGT. STANLEY J. DUKESHERER, KISKA, ALEUTIAN ISLANDS, ALASKA, 1945.** After the war, weatherman and wing-gunner Dukesherer would eventually leave his native Michigan for Westchester, purchasing his first home just a few doors from the Centinela Adobe. A grocer by trade, his first local job was at the Piggly-Wiggly Market in Westchester. He later opened Shoppers Market at Lincoln and Manchester Boulevards; now Ralph's Market. (Complements, John M. Wilson).

**HOWARD HUGHES.** Howard Hughes at the controls of his HK-1 Hercules flying boat. Following page, the HK-1(see next page), on it's maiden flight. (Complements, LAPL).

**SPRUCE GOOSE BEING TRANSPORTED TO LONG BEACH.**
On Jefferson Boulevard, the planes fuselage is being towed to Long Beach, where it was reassembled. (Complements, LAPL).

**LOYOLA CHAPEL.** Chapel of the Sacred Heart, Loyola University of Los Angeles, September 19, 1953. Loyola Marymount University is home to six spaces designed for Catholic worship. From the Spanish gothic Chapel of the Sacred Heart to architect Frank Gehry's post-modern Chapel of the Advocate, the university boasts some of the most beautiful and eclectic worship spaces in all of Los Angeles. Though all of the chapels are privately owned and operated by Loyola Marymount, their doors have always been open to the people of the greater university community. (Complements, LAPL) . Below, Chapel Interior. (Complements, LMU).

**BARBARA OWENS, (MRS. JOHN B. OWENS), 2009.** Artist and long time Westchester resident, Barbara Owens; "Sacred Heart, Chapel"-Loyola Marymount University. This stunning , limited edition watercolor, is presented here in black and white. #7 of 50 of the limited edition of this painting, hangs on the wall above the authors workspace. (Complements, Barbara A. Owens).

**LOS ANGELES TIME, JUNE 9, 1941.** (Courtesy, LAPL).

**NORTH AMERICAN STRIKE.** The corner of Inglewood-Redondo Road (now called Aviation Boulevard), and Imperial Avenue, the "hot spot" where teeming masses fought with tear gas and fists yesterday, is shown today--- practically a No Man's Land. The troops kept pickets a mile from the strikebound North American Aviation plant, and only those with business at the plant could pass through the area. The United States Army took over the factory on orders of President Roosevelt, who said defense plane production must go on. Photo dated: June 10, 1941. (Courtesy, LAPL).

**NORTH AMERICAN AIRCRAFT READY FOR A FIGHT, 1941.** This picture, first to be taken under a special permit from the War Department, shows why it is necessary to complete the Municipal Airport. British training ships are lined up on the ramp ready for delivery to Canada. At the left on the runway is an Army medium bomber awaiting its turn for a test. In the foreground are U.S. Army trainers for which there is no room on the ramp. The jam has made it necessary to enforce rigid traffic rules. (Courtesy, LAPL).

*A combination of the best minds in the world designing and building aircraft and a world war with high demand for aircraft, attracted what became the "people" who made up the fabric of the Westchester community. The Physical and social planning for Westchester intertwined with an emphasis on neighborhood consciousness and a sense of belonging, became the underpinnings of a thriving community that has endured the unprecedented growth of an airport leading into the 21st century as a world class aviation center.*

*--Mary Lou Crocket*

**MINES FIELD, 1941.** This photo of the Municipal Airport, the first to be taken under special permission of the War Department illustrates the necessity of completing the airport project for national defense. The field is overcrowded with new planes. Most of these are United States Navy trainers ready for final tests. At extreme right are two trainers for the British awaiting delivery to Canada. An average of 30 test hops is made daily at the uncompleted airport. (Courtesy, LAPL).

**NORTH AMERICAN AVIATION.** Inside and outside the strikebound North American Aviation plant, soldiers stood guard under orders from President Roosevelt, to see that the workers who returned to their jobs be afforded every protection. Photo shows men inside the vast plant working on training planes for the British. The factory is being run entirely by the Army. Photo dated: June 10, 1941. (Courtesy, LAPL).

**CROSSING THE PICKET LINES.** Army pilots are shown walking through the gates of the strikebound North American Aviation plant, after the picket line opened for them. They and other fliers will take delivery of nine completed planes and fly them to Kelly Field in Texas. Photo dated: June 5, 1941. (Courtesy, LAPL).

**JIMMY DOOLITTLE AT WESTCHESTER.** "This is Shangri-La! This is where B-25 bombers came from!" Brig. Gen. Jimmy Doolittle, the man who led that daring raid on Tokyo, told this cheering throng of aircraft workers at the North American plant. Photo dated: June 1, 1942. (Courtesy, LAPL)

**SOME WORKERS CROSS LINES.** Men are shown going through the gate to return to work on defense planes after the Army cleared away pickets. About 2002 men returned to their jobs at the North American aviation plant. Photo dated: June 9, 1941. (Courtesy, LAPL).

**MARTIAL LAW.** Some of the more than 3000 troops at the strikebound North American Aviation plant are shown at their camp on the grounds, lining up for chow. The Army set up machine gun posts (below), and used armored cars to clear the way for returning workers. The United States Army took over the factory on orders of President Roosevelt, who said defense plane production must go on. Photo dated: June 10, 1941. (Courtesy, LAPL).

**VIOLENT STRIKE.** Police officers are shown seizing a man during the fighting on the picket lines outside the strikebound North American Aviation plant. The riot started after Mayor Bowron ordered police to clear the gates. Photo dated: June 9, 1941. (Courtesy, LAPL).

**BAYONET READY.** Army troops enter the gates at the strikebound North American Aviation plant in Westchester The United States Army took over the factory on orders of President Roosevelt, who said defense plane production must go on. Photo dated: June 10, 1941.(Courtesy, LAPL).

**BACK TO WORK BOYS!** The last of the strikers are shown filing through a gate at the airplane plant which produces one-fifth of the United States' planes. Steel-helmeted troops stand guard to keep away possible picket line. Seven thousand workers of the day shift were back on the Job, turning out war planes under direct Army supervision. Photo dated: June 11, 1941. (Courtesy, LAPL).

**UNDER GUARD.** Guarded by soldiers with fixed bayonets, men who returned to work are shown putting finishing touches to advanced training planes for the Army Air Corps on the outdoor assembly plant at the factory. Photo dated: June 10, 1941. (Courtesy, LAPL).

**THREATENED WITH DRAFT IF THEY DO NOT RETURN TO WORK**.
This is today's "hot corner" on Imperial Avenue, a mile from the
strikebound North American Aviation plant, where strikers gather to
discuss the situation. Slight brushes marked the opening of the plant for
the day shift, but mostly all was peaceful. Photo dated: June 10, 1941.
(Courtesy, LAPL).

EL SEGUNDO DIVISION
DOUGLAS OWNED . . . . . . . 666,000 SQ. FT.
GOVERNMENT OWNED . . . 4,219,000 SQ. FT.

**MASSIVE DOUGLAS AIRCRAFT PLANT, EL SEGUNDO.** World War II was a major earner for Douglas. The company produced almost 30,000 aircraft from 1942 to 1945 and the workforce swelled to 160,000. The company produced a number of aircraft including the C-47 (based on the DC-3), the DB-7 (known as the A-20, Havoc or Boston), the Dauntless and the A-26 Invader. Lower photo; Workers Building SBD Dauntless Dive Bombers at Douglas Aircraft Plant Aircraft factory; workers build SBD Dauntless dive bomber engines at the Douglas aircraft plant in El Segundo, California. August 1943. (Courtesy, Google Books).

**KNUTE ROCKNE, ALL AMERICAN, (1940), WESTCHESTER.** Scenes from "Knute Rockne-All American," 1940. Ronald Reagan as George Gipp-HB, at Sullivan Field, Loyola University. The film featured Glen "Pop" Warner as himself. Note the trees growing along 80th Street, which have grown considerably since 1940. The biographical film which tells the story of Knute Rockne, Notre Dame football coach and perhaps the most famous of all coaches in college football history, for one of the most successful football programs in history. It stars Pat O'Brien, Ronald Reagan, Gale Page, Donald Crisp, Albert Bassermann, Owen Davis, Jr., Nick Lukats, Kane Richmond, William Marshall and William Byrne. It also included a cameo by legendary football coach Amos Alonzo Stagg, who played himself. The role of "George 'The Gipper' Gipp" by Ronald Reagan gave him the nickname of "The Gipper" for the rest of his life. (Complements, Google Books).

**ROBIN HOOD AT WESTCHESTER; ERROL FLYNN.**
Flynn and first wife Lili Damita at Los Angeles airport in 1941.
(Courtesy, Los Angeles Public Library).

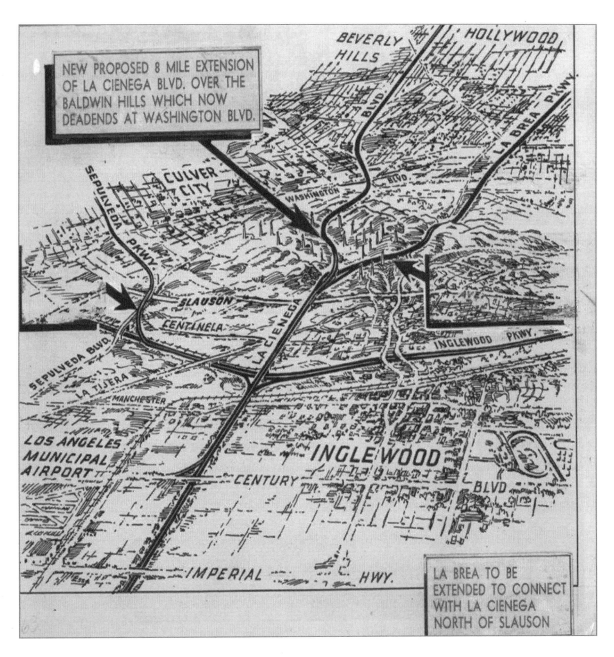

NEW PROPOSED 8 MILE EXTENSION OF LA CIENEGA BLVD. OVER THE BALDWIN HILLS WHICH NOW DEADENDS AT WASHINGTON BLVD.

LA BREA TO BE EXTENDED TO CONNECT WITH LA CIENEGA NORTH OF SLAUSON

**THE "NEVER BUILT" NEW FREEWAY, 1948.** This freeway was built in the late 1940's and was planned to be a part of the SR-170 Laurel Canyon Freeway. That freeway was never built past the Hollywood Freeway (US 101). When the La Cienega Blvd. Freeway was originally constructed, it probably had only four lanes. No mileposts or signs exist from the original construction. It is not even signed as a freeway anymore. Only two grade separated intersections at Slauson Avenue and the Baldwin Hills Park were constructed. The original structure looked similar to most 1940's bridges in CA. The segment that still has the access control runs from Rodeo Road on the north to Fairview Blvd on the south. (Courtesy, LAPL).

*Home builders such as Silas Nowell, Bert Farrar, Frank Ayers, Fred W. Marlow and Fritz B. Burns converged upon Westchester and built 3232 homes by 1943. The 3,000 acre community had been master planned by Security Bank. The bankers and the builders knew how to get the financing and produce housing for the defense workers.*

*--Mary Lou Crocket*

**WESTCHESTER, 1947.** Forty G.I.'s and their families will "invade" new homes in a caravan of 40 moving vans and autos at the Kaiser Community Homes projects in the Westchester district of southwest Los Angeles. The homes have but recently been completed and will be ready for occupancy when the hegira arrives with utilities men standing by to even turn on the gas, lights and water. According to Fritz B. Burns, President of the Kaiser Community Homes project, which has rushed these homes to completion for the mass moving in, this is the first good news of the year on housing shortages as it signifies the fast construction of homes now being accomplished. Ten homes are being built a day, with ten thousand of these homes scheduled to be built during the year. Cost per home varies slightly in the different tracks, with all substantially below $10,000 figured on the basis of $615.00 down and approximately $55.00 a month payment on them. Photo dated: February 24, 1947.(Courtesy, LAPL).

**1947 RUSETTA COUPE CLUB, INGLEWOOD.** Rusetta Coupe Club members and brothers Bob and Dick Pierson of Inglewood, California ran their '34 Ford 3-Window Coupe at the Dry Lakes. It was their daily transportation, as their mother thought it would be a safe car for them to drive, but eventually, over the ensuing years they sneaked it up to 140.40. It was no longer their daily driver. For the 1950 Dry Lakes Season at El Mirage, they stood the Hot Rod World on its ear when they figured out how to chop the top, lay back the windshield and yet still meet the SCTA's 7-inch windshield height regulation. Powered by a Bobby Meeks-built, Edelbrock equipped Flathead Merc, The Pierson Bros. 2D coupe consistently ran 150 mph. (Complements, Google).

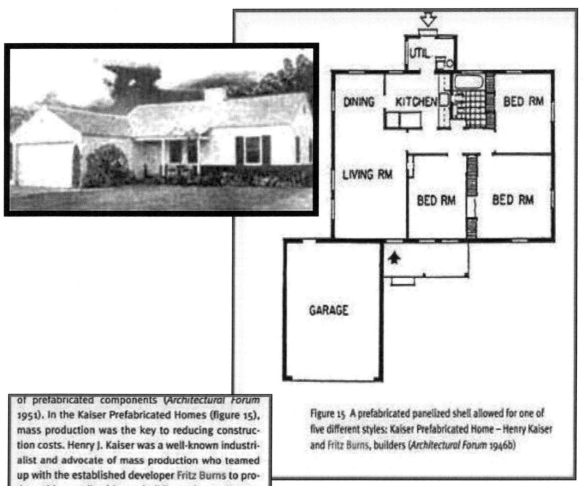

of prefabricated components (*Architectural Forum* 1951). In the Kaiser Prefabricated Homes (figure 15), mass production was the key to reducing construction costs. Henry J. Kaiser was a well-known industrialist and advocate of mass production who teamed up with the established developer Fritz Burns to produce this panelized home-building scheme. Factory production included full-wall, floor, and ceiling panels, plumbing equipment, kitchen cabinets, and a two-car garage. To avoid monotony, the houses were varied in appearance; site crews applied one of five "dressings": Cape Cod, Colonial, Ranch House, California, and Contemporary. The 90m² (900 ft²) homes could be purchased for $6,950 to $8,650 (*Architectural Forum* 1946b).

Figure 15 A prefabricated panelized shell allowed for one of five different styles: Kaiser Prefabricated Home – Henry Kaiser and Fritz Burns, builders (*Architectural Forum* 1946b)

## THE WESTCHESTER "GROW HOME"

Fritz Burns teamed up with Henry J. Kaiser to create low cost affordable housing in Westchester. The majority of the home was built off-site, and then transported to the building site. (Complements, Google Books).

**1929, BILL HANNON, AGE 16, AT LOYOLA HIGH SCHOOL.**
(Courtesy, William H. Hannon Foundation).

**WILLIAM H. HANNON.**
Born on October 2, 1913, in Los Angeles and died on November 4, 1999, in the same city he called home for a lifetime. He is remembered as a community builder whose passion for real estate was matched only by his passion for giving away the riches he had made.

William's father made his living as a rancher, and his mother was a homemaker. During the Great Depression when money was scarce, William's parents would put the children in their Studebaker and tour California's twenty-one Missions. This was not only an inexpensive form of entertainment, but it was also how William developed an interest in the history of early California and the Los Angeles area.

After graduating from Loyola High School in 1933, William wanted to attend Loyola University in Westchester (now Loyola Marymount University). With no money for a college education, William and his mother asked the President of Loyola University if they would admit him with the intention that William would pay back the school for his education once he got a job. William's college education began on a handshake deal that would result in his lifelong dedication and support of his alma mater. After his studies at Loyola University, William was called to serve as an intelligence officer in the Army. He received a special meritorious award for his work on the Manhattan Project, the group that designed and built the first atomic bomb.

In 1937 William began work with Fritz B. Burns & Associates. They subdivided thousands of acres in Westchester (along with Fred Marlow, Donald Ayres, Silas Nowell, and others), then built and sold homes to GIs returning from World War II. William Hannon and Fritz Burns then went on to develop sections of Playa del Rey, Panorama City, and Ontario. William continued in the real estate business independently of Fritz Burns, buying apartments, industrial buildings, and operating the popular San Fernando Swap Meet. He also served as president of the Fritz B. Burns Foundation, founded by his former partner and mentor.

Developer Fritz B. Burns, right, points out changes to friends who knew area when it was bean field. From left: J. Paul Campbell Sr., realtor Donald Ayres, co-developer Fred Marlow, and Charles Getchell.

**EXCERPT FROM THE LOS ANGELES HERALD EXAMINER, April 12th, 1963; THE BIRTH OF WESTCHESTER.** (Courtesy, David Coffin).

In 1939, plans for the areas first subdivision were submitted to the Los Angeles Planning Commission. The first housing unit was begun late in 1940. The delay was caused by the commission's concern over the proposed subdivision proximity to the 640-acre airport and it's lone 2200-foot landing strip.

Silas Nowell, the pioneer subdivider, was required to put up a number of houses before the Federal Housing Administration approved the area for residential loans with FHA backing. Los Angeles City Hall was then, as it is today , 10 miles from the northeast corner of Sepulveda and Manchester, where Nowell built his houses.

Not far behind Nowell came the firm of Marlow and Burns with ideas of its own about subdividing the acreage. Fred W. Marlow was a recently-resigned FHA director for California. Fritz B. Burns was an experienced realtor and subdivider, then best known for his development of Playa del Rey.

"There wasn't much here in 1941," Burns said the other day. He was seated in a private dining room of Westchester's new Airport-Marina Hotel, built and owned by Burns. "Charlie Crawford stirred our interest in starting an operation here," Burns continued, "and the first thing Fred Marlow and I knew, we were committed to take on 1400 acres. The price was around $1100 an acre and the bank was glad to see us.

"You wonder why an area like this remains dormant for so many years. The answer is that the distance from one place to another isn't measured in miles, but by the amount of intervening vacant territory. There was plenty between Westchester and downtown in those days, so Westchester was considered a long way out."

Cont.

On December 6th, 1941, Marlow finished pouring foundations for the first batch of Marlow-Burns houses.

"Fred called me the next morning and asked whether I thought we ought to go ahead with the development," Burns recalled. "I hadn't heard about the bombing of Pearl Harbor, so I said 'sure, why not?' Then he told me."

Burns decided to proceed with construction. Events proved this to be a wise decision.

When the war came to an end in 1945, Westchester was ripe and ready to grow to meet the demands of immediate and long-range postwar eras. Burns, Marlow and other developers became very busy.

**MAP, 1946.** Historic Roads to Romance: California's Southern Empire, Creator: Claude George Putnam. (Complements, LAPL).

**1946, LAX.** Actress Marlene Dietrich exiting airplane at Los Angeles International Airport, after entertaining troops during World War II. (Complements, LAPL). (Publication: Los Angeles Daily News - Publication date: August 8, 1946).

## PATMARS DRIVE-IN, MOTEL AND RESTAURANT-1940's

Driving along Sepulveda Boulevard near LAX today, it's hard to believe that there was ever so much vacant land; but this photo of Patmars Drive-In, at Sepulveda Boulevard and Imperial Highway, shows us just how much LAX has grown up since then.

For many years Patmars was a favorite stop for locals and tourists alike, but was probably most frequented by the Douglas Aircraft company employees. With plants all over Southern California, including Santa Monica and LAX, World War II was a major earner for Douglas. The company produced almost 30,000 aircraft from 1942 to 1945 and the workforce swelled to 160,000. The company produced a number of aircraft including the C-47 (based on the DC-3), the DB-7 (known as the A-20, Havoc or Boston), the Dauntless and the A-26 Invader. Local folks speak about Patmars in an American-Graffiti sort-of homage; a place where local high school kids took their dates for a soda and a burger, before and after a little cruising on Lincoln or Hawthorne Boulevard. (Postcard, Complements, Author).

**MILLIRON'S DEPARTMENT STORE, GRAND OPENING, 1949.**
1949 LA Herald Examiner: "Exterior view of the new modern Milliron's store in Westchester. The unique display houses are set at an angle for the benefit of auto traffic on Sepulveda Boulevard. Exterior view of the new Milliron's store in Westchester on March 17, 1949. A large crowd was drawn to official opening ceremonies at the store on Sepulveda Boulevard near Manchester." If you look closely at the upper-right section of the photograph, you can see the Loyola Theatre. (Courtesy Los Angeles Public Library).

**MILLIRON"S DEPARTMENT STORE, 1949.** It was in this display house beginning in the 1960's, that the Westchester Santa Claus would greet kids each Christmas season . The Terrace Restaurant windows can be seen near the top of the building. (Courtesy Los Angeles Public Library).

**THE BROADWAY WESTCHESTER.** The former Milliron's location traces its roots to one of the most prolific architects in history; sometimes credited with "inventing," and called the Father of the shopping mall: immigrant Victor Gruen. Gruen escaped Nazi occupied Austria in 1938, and eventually came to California with his new wife, and co-worker, Elsie Krummeck. They eventually designed the location, and began a lifelong successful career in designing shopping centers. This building was his first major project. Many new innovations were created here, including the angled display houses; angled so that passing cars could see the clothing and other goods on display. Below, the La Tijera Boulevard entrance to the rooftop parking and restaurant. Below right, memorial plaque; sadly , with graffiti (Courtesy, LAPL).

**DEL REY HILLS, 1928.** From Pershing Drive to the borders of Inglewood, all of the area we know today as Westchester and Playa Vista, was set aside for farming, although some oil exploration had begun on the Del Rey Bluffs and Wetlands. (Complements, Scripholy).

**ELLA DROLLINGER.** With sons Bob and Howard.

**HOWARD DROLLINGER.** Founded in 1947, H.B. Drollinger Co. (H.B.D. Co.) serves as the oldest and largest property management and commercial real estate brokerage firm in Westchester's Central Business District, adjacent to Los Angeles International Airport, the nation's third-busiest airport. The father of two, Mr. Drollinger was a longtime resident of Westchester. He flew 50 successful combat missions as navigator in a B-24 Liberator, 15th A.F., Italy. He was awarded the Distinguished Flying Cross, Purple Heart, four air medals and a Presidential Unit Citation while serving in the Army Air Force during World War II. (PHOTOS, Complements, H.B. Drollinger, Co.).

*On May 19, 1950, the City Council designated Los Angeles Airport as Los Angeles International (LAX). Westchester's Central Business District, located between Sepulveda Blvd. and 92nd Street, was "master planned" by Security Bank to keep up with the needed services of the "people" who came to live in the homes and work at the jobs. Ella L. Drollinger, the mother of Howard B. Drollinger, was one of the pioneer developers of the commercial real estate in Westchester. Since then, the H.B. Drollinger Co., under the direction of Howard Drollinger, has persevered in meeting the commercial needs of the "people" that live, work and play in our chamber service area.*
*--Mary Lou Crocket*

**MARY LOU CROCKET.** It would be difficult to tell an historical account of Westchester without remembering Mary Lou Crocket; founder of the Westchester/Playa Del Rey Historical Society. Raised in Westchester, graduating from Westchester High School and U.C.L.A. Mary Lou had been a local realtor since 1963, starting with the family firm of Otto Cripps Realty. This became Cripps Crockett Realtors in 1967. In 1992, Cripps Crockett Realtors transformed into Cripps Crockett Connection, a three-generation family firm, under the business umbrella of RE/MAX.

A former City of Los Angeles Library Commissioner and former member of the Board of Airport Commissioners, Mary Lou was widely recognized as a font of historic information about the Westchester community and one of the community's most involved citizens.

Mary Lou served on numerous boards, associations and committees as follows: Cofounder of Community Plans, Inc. – President 1968 to 1974,  Cofounder of Friends of the Library – Westchester/Loyola Village, President of the Board of Airport Commissioners, City of Los Angeles from 1980 to 1981, and member of the board, 1979-1984, President of the California Library Trustees and Commissioners from 1989 to 1990,  Honorary Mayor of Westchester in 1989-1990,  Commissioner to the City of Los Angeles Board of Library Commissioners from 1984–1993,  Loyola Marymount University's Continuing Education Advisory Board, Chairperson and Founder of the Westchester/Playa del Rey Historical Society – 1989 to present, President of Westchester Vitalization Corporation.,  Treasurer of the Neighborhood Council's Steering Committee for Westchester/Playa del Rey.

Cont.

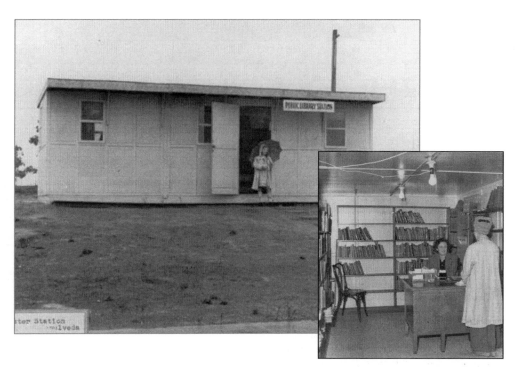

**FIRST LIBRARY.** Westchester Station, located at 86th Street and Kittyhawk Avenue, before establishment of the Westchester Branch in July 1952, of the Los Angeles Public Library. (Courtesy, LAPL).

Mary Lou simply was Westchester," said Gwen Vuchsas, President of the Neighborhood Council of Westchester/Playa del Rey. "She will always be a part of this community because she gave so much to it during her life."

In 2003, Mary Lou was honored with the Fritz B. Burns Outstanding Community Service Award, which commemorated Burns' own lifelong dedication to community-building and honors individuals who have served as outstanding role models for community leadership. The award included a check, which Crockett promptly distributed to the Friends of the Library-Westchester/Loyola Village; the Westchester Fourth of July Parade; and the Westchester/Playa del Rey Historical Society. She was a benevolent financial contributor to many, many non-profit organizations.

Always looking to better the community, she started the Westchester Fourth of July Parade in 2000 as part of the Historical Society's celebration of the millennium (previous page photo of Tony P's float). That annual event now draws thousands of local residents to celebrate the nation's birth.

# *Five*
## NEW DEVELOPMENTS

Up and down all of the boulevards of Westchester, commerce was booming, as stores of all kinds opened to support the new region. Life was good. Grocery stores such as Piggly-Wiggly, Hillmart, Dorr's, Von's, Safeway, Ralph's, and Mayfair Markets, opened.

Sav-on, J.C. Penney, Woolworth's and Newberry's, all opened on Sepulveda Boulevard, creating *Uptown* Westchester. The lunch counters at Woolworth's and Newberry's are fondly remembered by many.

Three theatres opened; the Loyola and the Paradise; on Sepulveda Boulevard, and the La Tijera on La Tijera Boulevard. The towns first bowling alley; Paradise Bowl opened.

Specialty stores such as Hy Greens Sporting Goods, Ray's Pet Shop, De Luca Jewelers, Monroe's Men's Wear, See's Candies, and Thom McCann Shoes, were all anchored by the newly built Milliron's Department Store. Milliron's would be sold to Broadway Stores a few years later.

The 1950's began a long standing tradition with local well-heeled ladies and their daughters, who donned white gloves and went to tea atop the Broadway Westchester at the Terrace Restaurant; and then perhaps to see a matinee.

Out on Lincoln Boulevard, Fritz Burns opened the Airport Marina Hotel, and across the street , the Fireside grill and piano bar. And just as on Sepulveda Boulevard, all sorts of businesses sprang up. Across the street, a new municipal park was erected; complete with a swimming center.

Restaurants and diners such as the Cavalier, the Buggy Whip, the Trails, the Bar of Melody, Bryan's Pitt Bar-B-Q, and the Galley Café, were opened. Down the hill, in a carnival –like setting, the Airport Village opened, and at Hamburger Handout, burgers were .19 cents. Across the street, Dinah's Family Restaurant opened. Another Handout opened on Manchester near Airport Boulevard.

Service Stations, Laundries and dry cleaners, stationary stores, delicatessens, cobblers and tailors, and hardware stores were opening on every corner. Where before you had to travel to Inglewood, *Crenshaw* or Downtown Los Angeles for goods and services, Westchester now could support it's townspeople.

**LAX; LABOR DAY AIRPORT "RUSH," 1953.** (Courtesy, LAPL).

At Sepulveda and Manchester Boulevards, hot rodders and poodle skirters had their meals roller skated to their automobile windows at a place called Tiny Naylor's Drive-In. Car clubs sprung up; cruising and street racing were the rage. People surfed in the summer months, and suped up their hot rods in the winter. But there was always plenty to do; the Clock Drive-in, the Centinela Drive-in; listening to KHJ and KRLA.

At a town that today supports just two Little League baseball programs, five Leagues; International, National, Del Rey, American and Lincoln Little Leagues were formed. You couldn't even buy a soccer ball in the area at this time. The Westchester YMCA opened and a gymnasium and tennis courts were erected at Westchester Recreation Center.

New schools and churches opened too; including a new high school. It was no longer necessary for teens to travel to Venice and Inglewood to attend those high schools. Westchester High School opened in 1948, at what is now Orville Wright Middle School; moving to the current site in 1957.

All sorts of civic and fraternal clubs were formed, including the Knights of Columbus, Lions, Elks, Rotary and a Chamber of Commerce. All up and down Aviation and Century Boulevards, new hotels were being built to support LAX and the new aerospace economy.

Loyola University Los Angeles continued to expand, becoming one of the top Jesuit American Colleges. Three large Catholic churches and parishes were founded; the Church of the Visitation and Grammar School, Saint Anastasia, and finally Saint Jerome's. Many other public schools were erected, including; Kentwood, Orville Wright, and Cowan Avenue schools.

Between 1947 and 1951, just past and above our towns borders, at a place built and named for horse racing pioneer Elias J. *"Lucky "* Baldwin, the Los Angeles Department of Water and Power erected the Baldwin Hills dam on an active fault line. The design consisted of four layers above the rock foundation: an asphalt lining, a gravel drain basin, compacted clay, and a final asphalt layer on the top. The fault lines were considered during planning.

To support the music minded youth in the area, Westchester Music Store opened, and two young teens, who would later become the rock group The Turtles, took music lessons there. Just next door, the first automatic car wash in the area opened, and next to that, the business advertised itself as a; "Chinese Laundry."

Every year the Westchester Community Fair would bring traffic at La Tijera and Sepulveda Boulevards to a near standstill, and each year a Miss Westchester was chosen from the lovely teenaged girls in the area.

Nearby Inglewood continued to grow at leaps and bounds, and boasted a vibrant downtown shopping area, many movie theaters and a championship country club; Inglewood Country Club. Next to the country club, a racetrack was built.

Hollywood Park was opened in 1938 by the Hollywood Turf Club. The racetrack was designed by noted racetrack architect Arthur Froehlich. Its chairman was Jack Warner of Warner Brothers, and its 600 shareholders included many other Hollywood luminaries. Al Jolson and Raoul Walsh were members of the founding Board of Directors and Mervyn LeRoy was a director from 1941 until his death in 1987.

The Academy Theatre in Inglewood, built by Cecile B. De Mille, was intended to be the permanent site of the Academy Awards Gala, but plans were shelved when Hollywood stars refused to make the" long drive" to the region. In 1941, future actress Jean Craig finished her sophomore year at Inglewood High School. In 1946, George Foster founded Foster's Freeze on La Brea Avenue; a location that still remains as the first fast-food chain in the state.

The Red and Yellow Street Cars still serviced the region surrounding Westchester, but by the time the town received it's name, the automobile was king, and tracks were never laid through the town. And despite it's ever growing population, the town remained a remote and often forgotten Westside village. All of this would change with The Federal-Aid Highway Act of 1956, popularly known as the National Interstate and Defense Highways Act (Public Law 84-627), was enacted on June 29, 1956, when President Dwight D. Eisenhower signed the bill into law.

Eisenhower's support of the Federal-Aid Highway Act of 1956 can be directly attributed to his experiences in 1919 as a participant in the U.S. Army's first Transcontinental Motor Convoy across the United States on the historic Lincoln Highway, which was the first paved highway across America. This is how Lincoln Boulevard was named. The highly publicized 1919 convoy was intended, in part, to dramatize the need for better main highways and continued federal aid. The convoy left the Ellipse south of the White House in Washington D.C. on July 7, 1919, and headed for Gettysburg, Pennsylvania. From there, it followed the Lincoln Highway to San Francisco. Bridges cracked and were rebuilt, vehicles became stuck in mud, and equipment broke, but the convoy was greeted warmly by communities across the country. The convoy reached San Francisco on September 6, 1919.

With the expansion and retrofitting of local freeways, including the San Diego Freeway, (Route 405); which roughly creates the eastern border of Westchester, commutes between urban centers to suburbs such as Westchester were much quicker, furthering the flight of citizens and businesses and divestment from inner cities, and compounding vehicle pollution and excessive petroleum use problems.

And suddenly, the region exploded.

With little fanfare, the street-car trolleys of Los Angeles stopped running in 1959. With the exception of the San Diego Freeway, extended through the region in the 1960's, and built along the creek beds of Centinela Springs and over the vast vineyards and fruit orchards that once existed there, no new north/south road infrastructure had been created since the mission friars had built the El Camino Real.

The former wagon roads, cattle trails and coastal drives: Lincoln and Sepulveda Boulevards, and Vista Del Mar along the ocean, became the new commuting roads in the area, as the San Diego Freeway, and the unimaginable congestion that occurs there, was regularly reduced to a parking lot.

Roads were widened and re-routed, but they are still the same old roads. And although rapid transit buses were expanded throughout the region, nothing could replace the now defunct trolley car system that once helped to sustain the region.

LAX traffic: both aircraft and automobile, increased ten times over twenty years. Just south of LAX, the sleepy beach communities of Manhattan Beach, El Segundo and Hermosa Beach were experiencing explosive population growth as well. Manhattan Beach had grown at a rate of 170.9% between 1940 and 1950, and then doubled that growth between 1950 and 1960; to over 34,000 souls.

In Los Angeles in general, between 1940 and 1960, the population grew from 2.8 million to over 6 million people. By 2000, these numbers increased to almost 9.9 million. This growth has dramatically affected land use as homes, buildings, and roads have been built upon what was once open land.

Between 1948 and 1998, passenger traffic a LAX grew from 1.2 million passengers to 44 million passengers, and 60 million by 2008. Just as passengers have to travel local roads to get to and from their flights, trucks need to deliver and or pick up shipments. LAX cargo, increased from 16,000 tons in 1948, to 1.1 million tons in 1998, and again, most of this was occurring on the same roads.

The Westchester/Del Rey Bluff area, adjacent to the Ballona Wetlands and the Howard Hughes company, existed on the northern edge of Playa Del Rey as a land and nature buffer, and a drainage area and safety zone against documented monumental flooding. As a result, one of the last inland marsh ecosystems, anywhere in California, sustained an unofficial sanctuary for coastal wildlife and many endangered species of plant life.

The 1950's, sometimes called; *The Apathetic 50's*, ended, ushering in the 1960's and a new race for the moon, partially engineered by the scientists and aerospace experts housed and/or working at Westchester.

Virtually every practical area in Westchester had been developed or was in planned subdivision, except for one large farm on Manchester Boulevard; soon to be made into the towns golf course. Neighborhoods were named; Kentwood, Westport Heights, Manchester Square, and Osage, to name a few.

As the economy of the mid-1930's began to improve, and with the National Housing Act of 1934; the Federal Housing Administration (FHA) was created, development soared. It was established primarily to increase home construction and reduce unemployment, and made it possible for first time home buyers to purchase a home.

And now the post war GI's could buy a home with their benefits from the GI Bill. The bill which President Roosevelt initially proposed was not as far reaching. The G.I. Bill was created to prevent a repetition of the Bonus March of 1932 and a relapse into the Great Depression after World War II ended.

An important provision of the G.I. Bill was low interest, zero down payment home loans for servicemen. This enabled millions of American families to move out of urban apartments and into suburban homes. Prior to the war the suburbs tended to be the homes of the wealthy and upper class.

But developers such as Fritz Burns had made it easy for anyone to own a home in the suburb of Westchester. At one time Kentwood homes sold for $150.00 down, and $150.00 a month. At one point, home buying reached such a feverish pace that lotteries were held. And to insure that their children could get a desk at some of Westchester's new public schools, parents sometimes camped out on the school steps to be first in line on registration days.

Again, as Westchester entered the 1960's, everything seemed perfect in the town. Jobs were plentiful, services and infrastructure were dependable, there was plenty of clean air and drinking water; and new generation would soon take the torch, leading an ever expanding- proud Nation into a new Space Age.

Local pride was exemplified all over Westchester, with a unique local custom; the Westchester Christmas Candle. Local residents began to purchase or home-build tall eight-foot red Christmas Candles, and anchor them in the lawns in front of their homes during Christmastime. At one time hundreds if not thousands existed. Small signs with seasons greetings or the homeowner names were placed in front of the candles, and illuminated by spotlights. With each stake and anchor laid into the ground, it was as if the resident was proclaiming his pride for and place in the town.

But strange things were happening all over Southern California in 1959; the warmest year in recorded history. On and around the Bluff- town of Westchester, the next decade would change the complexion of the face of the town forever.

**1948, CENTINELA SCHOOL CLASS.** Centinela School First 1st Grade Class Picture - March 30 1948. (Complements, Google Books).

**1947, CENTINELA SCHOOL CLASS.** Centinela School A.M. Kindergarten Class Picture - June 20 1947. (Complements, Google Books).

**INGLEWOOD,
MATCHBOOK HISTORY.**
Frank Afton Studebaker,
Inglewood Country Club,
Boot's and Saddle
Restaurant, Yum Burger,
Edmundson Trailer Service.
(Complements, Author).

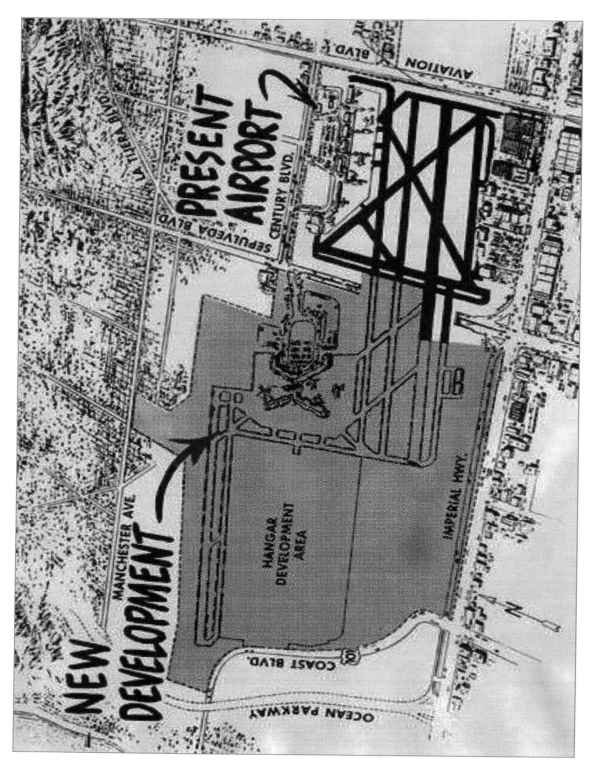

**1951 ARTISTS CONCEPTION, LAX.** In this version, the airport would extend through what we today call Westchester Park and Westchester Golf Course , and all the way to Manchester Boulevard and Emerson Avenue. This plan was never approved, but later development did indeed condemn many homes in this section of Westchester. (Courtesy, LAPL).

**DON KLOSTERMAN; THE DUKE OF DEL REY.** Don Klosterman earned the nickname "The Duke of Del Rey" while playing quarterback for the Lions. Bud Furillo explains in his tribute to Klosterman, "In our first conversation, he [Klosterman] chose to talk with me about the Duke Ellington Orchestra. Thus he became 'The Duke of Del Rey.' " Klosterman was the leader of the 1950 Loyola team that, using Head Coach Jordan Oliver's rare passing game, came within a 28-26 upset loss to Santa Clara of going to the Orange Bowl. With Oliver's system in place, Klosterman used his passing ability to set single-game and season records for passes attempted and completed. He set the mark for most passing yards over a three-year span with 4,481. Loyola discontinued football following the 1951 season, and Olivar was hired on as a part-time assistant at Yale. PHOTO, the 1950 Loyola University Lions, (8-1), at Sullivan Field, Westchester, CA. (Complements, Google). Inset, 1950 Football Program, vs. St. Mary's. (Complements, Authors Collection).

**HAMBURGER HANDOUT.** A sign at the left of James Collins' original Hamburger Handout stand advertises 10-cent hamburgers in celebration of its sixth anniversary in this 1958 photo. The 19-cent burger chain that eventually grew to four outlets began in 1952. Founder James Collins had studied the new hamburger operation that New Hampshire brothers; Richard and Maurice, McDonald had begun in San Bernardino on December 12, 1948. He decided to use their concept for his own version, Hamburger Handout, which opened at the corner of Sepulveda and Centinela boulevards near the Culver City/Westchester border in October 1952. The Handout's 19-cent hamburger soon became a fixture in the area, so much so that alumni Web sites from four different nearby high schools; Culver City, Hawthorne, El Segundo and Westchester, have postings from 1950s grads who fondly remember it. Collins opened the additional restaurants in the Hamburger Handout chain in 1957, 1958 and 1960. In any case, by the early 1960s, Collins had begun to abandon the concept after meeting up with Col. Harlan Sanders over this new fried chicken concept and closed the Hamburger Handouts down. As a result of the Sanders discussions, in 1962 Collins became the exclusive agent for Kentucky Fried Chicken outlets in Southern California. By the mid-1960s his group owned more than 200 KFC outlets in the West. McDonald's opened up one of their first restaurants in Westchester on La Tijera, just up the hill from the Hamburger Handout. (Complements, Sam Gnerre).

NIXON WELCOMED, 1952. Senator Richard Nixon came home on July 28, 1952, to greeters at Los Angeles International Airport included this group rallied around the Republican Club of El Segundo sign. Youngsters came along with their mamas to welcome the nominee for veep. (Courtesy, LAPL).

**1958, DODGER LANDING**; Photograph caption dated June 2, 1958 reads, "Never in the history of baseball did a team--a last place team--receive such a welcome as that accorded the Dodgers last night at International Airport, where some 7500 rabid fans met the club."

The Dodgers would reverse their disappointing 1958 season, winning the 1959 Pennant and taking the World Series from the Chicago White Sox.

**(This photograph, and the following pages of "LAX Arrivals/Departures," courtesy the Los Angeles Herald Examiner Collection, at the Los Angeles Public Library).**

**YVONNE DI CARLO;** arrives at Los Angeles Airport after flying in from Europe where she was linked romantically with Aly Kahn. She attended the International Film Festival at Cannes, and reports immediately to MGM to star in a picture there. Photo dated: June 7, 1952.

**AVA GARDNER AND FRANK SINATRA**; posed willingly for photographers at International Airport before boarding TWA Constellation en route to London to perform in a gigantic benefit show. Photo dated: December 7, 1951.

**VIA TWA**; a trio of Yankees stopped over here today en route to Japan. They are Billy Martin, reserve infielder; Joe DiMaggio, outfielder; and Ed Lopat, southpaw pitcher. DiMaggio is here visiting his son, Joe, Jr." Photograph dated: October 13, 1951.

## ERROL AND HIS GHEEK BACK IN HOLLYWOOD, 1950.

Photograph caption reads, "When dashing Errol Flynn of the movies returned to Hollywood with his Princess Ghica, who he affectionately calls 'Gheek,' he was greeted at the (International) airport in Westchester by not only his own mother, Mrs. Thompson Flynn (right), but also by his ex-mother-in-law, Mrs. Margaret Eddington (second from right), mother of his former wife, Nora Eddington Haymes. Princess (left) and Flynn plan to marry in September." Photograph dated: May 17, 1950.

**LANA TURNER, 1958**; Motion picture actress Lana Turner and escort Johnny Stompanato arriving at Los Angeles International Airport, with her daughter Cheryl Crane, later to be accused of killing him.

**1959 WELCOME:** Photograph caption dated October 3, 1959 reads, "Here are some of the 5000 greeters at airport last night as the Dodgers returned from Chicago where they evened the series yesterday. What a day it'll be at the Coliseum tomorrow!"

**HERE COME THE DODGERS!:** Photograph caption dated October 3, 1959 reads, "Here are some of the Dodger Fan Club enthusiasts at the airport last night in Westchester. They and all Southern Californians are now ready for the very first World Series Game ever to be played in Los Angeles. Coliseum will be rocking tomorrow!"

**MR AND MRS. WALTER O'MALLEY:** Refusing to make a prediction on the outcome of the World Series in Chicago and insisting "we're just hoping for a victory", Los Angeles Dodger President Walter O'Malley and his wife board their chartered United Air Lines' plane for the Windy City early this morning at Los Angeles International Airport in Westchester. Fifty-one Dodger executives, friends and players' wives were aboard the chartered plane. Photo dated: October 7, 1959.

**BOEING 707, 1959.** Passengers board a Boeing 707 airliner,. (Courtesy, LAPL).

**NEW TUNNEL.** Cars and trucks go through Sepulveda Airport Underpass in Westchester, in a final testing prior to the opening of the $3,500,000 tunnel. 1953.(Courtesy, LAPL).

**RUBENSTEIN'S PACIFIC COAST WAREHOUSE AND PLANT, EL SEGUNDO.**
Exterior view of Helena Rubenstein's half-million dollar Pacific Coast warehouse and plant. Building was just completed in El Segundo, Calif., to expedite service to the eleven western states. Said to be the largest cosmetic warehouse in the west, the building marks the fourth major expansion by Helena Rubenstein in the area in 15 years and is expected to aid the firm in doing record business. Photo dated: November 9, 1954. (Courtesy, LAPL).

**WESTCHESTER HIGH SCHOOL, 1957.** (Courtesy, Google Books).

**EL SEGUNDO BEACH SCENE, 1949.** Prior to El Segundo's incorporation in 1917, this area was part of "Rancho Sausal Redondo" ("*Ranch of the Round Clump of Willows*"), a rancho with a land mass of nearly 25,000 acres which extended from the areas as far north of what is now Playa del Rey, as far east as Inglewood, and as far south as Redondo Beach. The land consisted of wheat and barley fields on which cattle and sheep grazed. (Courtesy LAPL).

**1960, LAX/WESTCHESTER NEW CONSTRUCTION.** Control Tower (1) rises to its height of 172 feet as foundation of ticketing building (2) takes shape. Site preparation is 90 per cent complete two months ahead of schedule. The previous control tower at LAX was partially dismantled and moved to Riverside Raceway to be used by racing officials. (Courtesy, LAPL).

**A NEW THEME FOR LAX AND WESTCHESTER, 1960.** Huge steel arches are set in place for 'Theme Structure' of the Los Angeles International Airport. Don Belding, President of Board of Airport Commissioners, waves the flag signaling the placement of the 105-foot-long arches which give parabolic shape to the $2,200,000 building. The Theme Building is a landmark structure at the Los Angeles International Airport within the Westchester neighborhood of the city of Los Angeles. It opened in 1961, and is an example of the Mid-Century modern influenced design school known as "Googie" or "Populuxe." (Courtesy, LAPL).

**THE JETSONS**. The architecture shown in *The Jetsons* was based on the Theme Building's exterior; the Theme Building's interior was later redesigned to have a "Jetsons" feel. (Courtesy, *Wikipedia)*.

**THE PACIFIC ELECTRIC STREETCAR SYSTEM.** (Complements, United States Library of Congress).

**LOS ANGELES RED CAR, 1953.** This is PERY Car 5117 in Ocean Park near the end of the Air Line, or the beginning of the Inglewood Line. The line continued to Venice, Marina Del Rey, near Westchester, and Inglewood, on a private right-of-way along Neilson Way, Main St, Electric Ave near Abbot Kinney, north of Marina Del Rey, along the entrance of the Marina Freeway, Jefferson Blvd, and Centinela Ave. This part of the line wasn't called the Air Line but Inglewood Line. The Inglewood Line terminated at the BNSF Harbor Subdivision right-of-way in Inglewood. This was a Sunday charter trip and someone knew no regular trains ran on Sunday, so used the track for a parking lot. Dated July 17, 1953. (Complements, transitalk).

**LAX POSTCARD VIEWS.** One of the next terminals to open was Terminal Four used by American. The view above looks to the west on a very clear day. At the bottom of the frame, we see cars belonging to the construction workers at Western's Terminal Five. The current Bradley International Terminal occupies the site where the North/South crosswind runway is located immediately above the American terminal, and the area beyond is currently filled with hangars and remote gates. You can see Point Dume, the northern limit of Malibu, just under the "c" in "Pacific." (Authors 1950's era Postcard Collection).

**80TH STREET AND SEPULVEDA BOULEVARD, 1953.** Westchester Lutheran begins construction of new school classrooms. This view is from Sepulveda and 80th St. BELOW; 77th and Sepulveda Boulevard, 1953, looking southwest. (Courtesy, David Coffin).

THE NEW "Westchester"*

• THE 1936 PLYMOUTH with "Westchester" semi-sedan suburban body . . . the last word in utility and reliability, with
Plymouth economy and genuine Hydraulic Brakes. Full
glass enclosed . . . equipped with safety glass and window-
lift controls—or curtains. Rattle-proof seats for 7 to 8 passengers, on the best engineered chassis in the low-price
field. Ask any Dodge, De Soto or Chrysler dealer for details.

## By PLYMOUTH

* "Westchester" - Trade Mark Registered U. S. Pat. Off. by U. S. Bolt and Forging Co., Inc.

**1936 PLYMOUTH WESTCHESTER; FACTORY PRICE, $746.00**, I was once told that Charlie Crawford had named the town after a car that he particularly liked, but I have never been able to verify this. (Complements, Author).

**KENTWOOD PLAYERS**. Since 1949, the Kentwood Players have kept community theatre alive at the Westchester Playhouse, 8301 Hindry Avenue. The Playhouse is located just a few blocks from the historic Centinela Adobe. (Courtesy, Kentwood Players).

**THE LA Tijera THEATER, 1949.** The marquee is advertising; John Loves Mary, starring future California Governor and US President, Ronald Reagan. (Complements, Cinema Treasures).

**NEW YEARS DAY, 1947.** Lyons moving vans parked in the Westchester, CA housing development, in the Los Angeles area, showing massive amounts of post-war housing construction. (Courtesy, Life Magazine).

**LA Tijera THEATRE, 1942.** The marquee is advertising; *Ride "Em Cowboy,* with Bud Abbott, Lou Costello, and Dick Foran. (Complements, Cinema Treasures).

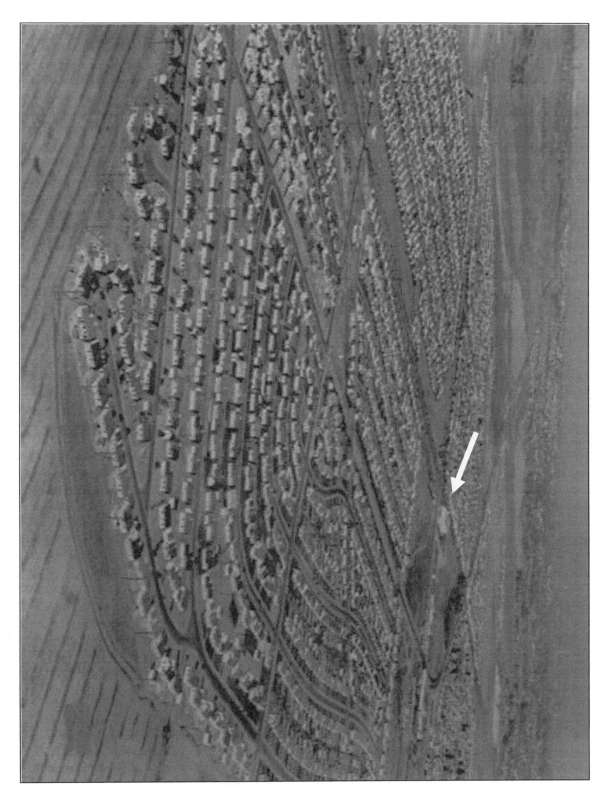

**WESTCHESTER, CALIFORNIA, 1948.** The arrow is pointing to the new Loyola Theatre, designed by Clarence J. Smale. (Courtesy, LAPL).

**AIRFREIGHT TERMINAL, HUGHES AIRPORT, WESTCHESTER.**
Tom Slick Airways, Hughes Airport, 1951. (Courtesy, David Coffin).

**THE BOB HOPE FAMILY, LAX, 1949.** (Courtesy, LAPL).

## THE TRAILS RESTAURANT, WESTCHESTER, CA, 1952.

The Trails was located down Sepulveda Hill, next to Dinah's Family Restaurant. It was a local haunt for Howard Hughes, and throughout the restaurant, animals were kept in cages. With Esther Williams and her husband, Ben Gage; Ray Darby, County Supervisor; Dick Renz, Fair Queen chairman. Officials of sixth annual Westchester Community Fair discuss plans for the selection of a queen who will reign over the Westchester Community Fair. (Complements, Los Angeles Public Library).

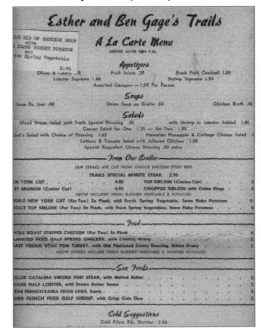

**ESTHER WILLIAMS.** Actress and world class swimmer. (Complements, Google).

**LIFE MAGAZINE, 1949.** Aerial view of acres of new homes, mostly in the $12,000 range, creating compact rows jammed together side-by-side along a wavy grid work of streets in a suburban area called Westchester. (Complements, Life Magazine).

**THE BUGGY WHIP,** 1949. One of Westchester's old standards, The Buggy Whip, formerly Petersons Buggy Whip, has operated on La Tijera Blvd. since 1949. It serves exceptional cuts of beef and seafood. It is also famous for its' Green Goddess dressing. The dressing is named for its green tint. The most accepted theory regarding its origins points to the Palace Hotel in San Francisco in 1923, when the hotel's executive chef wanted something to pay tribute to actor George Arliss and his hit play, *The Green Goddess.* He then concocted this dressing, which, like the play, became a hit. This dressing is a variation of a dressing originated in France by a Chef to Louis XIII who made a Sauce Au Vert (Green Sauce) which was traditionally served with 'Green Eel. (Courtesy, The Buggy Whip).

**FIRESIDE BAR AND GRILL, 1950.** Rumor is that Fritz Burns and his pals opened the Fireside so they could have a close-by quiet place to hold business dinners and lunches. It was at one point a fabulous piano bar. Whatever the truth, the Fireside has stood the test of time and operated continuously for sixty years; although was recently renamed; Tompkins Grill. It is a favorite hang-out for local residents and upper-classman from Loyola Marymount University. (Courtesy, yelp.com). Inset, Fritz Burns. (Courtesy, Life Magazine).

**WATERCOLOR; "HOME COOKING," BARBARA OWENS, 2010.** View of Dinah's Family Restaurant, Westchester, CA..The painting won first prize in the 2010 Pacific Art Guild competition. The Giant Tub Sign, displayed over the Take-Out Department was the very first Tub Sign in Los Angeles. The Tub is now recognized by many as the symbol for Dinah's Famous Fried Chicken. Dinah's Fried Chicken has received critical acclaim over the years as a superior food product, and is by far, the best fried chicken in Westchester. Dinah's first opened at the base of the Westchester Bluffs in 1959. The Collins Food's headquarters, which operated over 200 Col. Sanders diners, was just down the block from Dinah's, and it is highly probable that they got the ideas for the Kentucky Fried Chicken tub signs from Dinah's. (Complements, Barbara A. Owens).

**THE LOYOLA THEATRE**. This is a later 1960's image. Below, 1947 view of cinema interior. "Free Shows," were hosted here every summer by Marina Federal Savings and Loan. Candy across the street at Sav-On Drugs was three for ten cents; ice cream cones a nickel. (Complements, Author).

**COACH JORDAN OLIVAR, LOYOLA UNIVERSITY LIONS.** Jordan Olivar was born Giordano Aurelio Olivari in 1915, in Brooklyn, New York, the son of Italian immigrants. His father had jumped ship in New York, and later, Coach Olivar would enjoy telling people that his father was an early illegal alien. His father waited on tables and picked up a little money on the side as a boxer. In 1949, three years before football ended for good at Loyola, Coaches Jordan Olivar and Jerry Neri arrived to lead the school to its last gridiron glory with an aerial attack ahead of the times. By 1949, the new Loyola head coach, Jordan Olivar, and his top assistant, Jerry Neri, both in their mid-30s, had enjoyed great success in leading their alma mater, Villanova College of Philadelphia, to a 33-20-2 record during the previous six years. Olivar helped pioneer the Belly-T, or Belly Series (some people at the time called it the Drive Series or the Ride Series, but the name "Belly" won out). The Belly was the seeds of the Wishbone T (the name that won out over "Y" formation) that would come along almost a generation later. Although he had never played in a game of football until he arrived at Villanova, on a football scholarship, yet he wound up starring on some of the Wildcats' greatest teams, playing first for Harry Stuhldreher, one of Knute Rockne's legendary Four Horsemen, and then for Maurice "Clipper" Smith, another former Rockne player. For some reason, Coach Stuhldreher referred to him as "Olivar" and to his teammate Alex Belli as "Bell," and both men wound up anglicizing their names. (Complements, Google Books). Inset, program; Loyola vs. College of the Pacific, 9-29-1951. (Complements, Authors Collection).

**1959, CENTURY BOULEVARD'S NEW INTERNATIONAL HOTEL.**

**FRITZ BURN"S AIRPORT MARINA HOTEL,
LINCOLN AND MANCHESTER BOULEVARDS.**
(Photo's, Complements, Google).

**EMERSON MANOR KINDERGARTEN**. A group of mothers register their children for kindergarten at Westchester School. Photos dated: September 1, 1953. (Courtesy, LAPL).

**LONG NIGHT.**
Members of the Westchester School P.T.A. serve coffee and doughnuts to parents waiting to enroll their children at the Westchester kindergarten. Recent influx of new residents completely swamped city's school facilities. Photograph dated: September 13, 1948.

**FIRST COME, FIRST SERVED**. A long line of parents stand in front of Kentwood School in the Westchester district, waiting to enroll their children in kindergarten. They lined up at 2:30 p.m. yesterday and remained there all night. Today, many were turned away, disappointed, because the school could only admit 25 pupils. Photograph dated January 31, 1949.(Photos, Courtesy, LAPL).

# Youth Band Plans Party

WESTCHESTER — Westcester Youth Band members will hold their annual Christmas party and dinner at 6:15 p.m. Monday at Westchester Playground.

Howard Kaplan, master of ceremonies, will sing a song he wrote and will be accompanied by Jackie Waddel.

Other entertainment will be furnished by band members Mike Van Ourkirk, Jan Nichols, David Sheppard, Geoffry Bales, Gary Chase, Peggy Ishikawe, Nora Lynn Stevens, Lynette Fromme and Anne Marine Stafford.

Mrs. Gretchen Melvill, mother of a band member, will present a dance and Fern Jaros, former band director, will play a trombone solo.

**SQUEAKY CHRISTMAS PARTY, 1960.** "The Westchester Youth Band plans its Christmas party. Entertainment will be provided by band members Mike Van Ourkirk, Jan Nichols, David Sheppard, Geoffry Bales, Gary Chase, Peggy Ishikawe, Nora Lynn Stevens, Lynette Fromme and Anne Marine Stafford. Fern Jaros, former band director, will play a trombone solo". Lynette "Squeaky" Fromme would later become a Charles Manson follower, and attempted to assassinate President Gerald Ford. (Compliments, Daily Mirror).

**FLAG DAY.** Verona Cox, right, teacher of B-2 class at Westchester School, leads her pupils in the pledge of allegiance to the Flag as classes opened for an all-time high of 1,250,000 pupils for city and county schools. Photo dated: September 12, 1955. (Courtesy, LAPL).

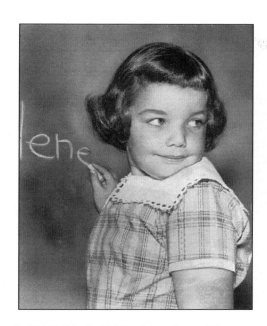

**SCHOOL DAYS.** Charlene Theroux, 7 years old, shows her teacher at Westchester School how well she can write her name on September 12, 1955.(Courtesy, LAPL).

**THE GIBBONS FAMILY, 1956.** Gibbons Kids - Eddie, Richie, Mattie, Paul and Patty; El Manor Avenue. Note the garbage incinerator in the rear of the yard. (Complements, Gibbons Family).

**EARLY CRUISERS.**
Sigfred Ponce de Leon, 5 years old, shown in center, proudly shows off his bike to new friend and future classmate, John Jessup, 5, at left, while his brother, Steven, 3, looks on, at Westchester School on September 7, 1955. (Courtesy, LAPL).

**LOCAL BOWLING CHAMPIONS.** Photo of Dick Jensen and Andy Marzich bowling together at La Tijera Bowl (formerly La Tijera Theatre). Dick and Andy won first place in the ABC doubles, 1960, and were members of the same team that won the 1960 California team championship. Andy also won Southern California Bowler of the Year title, 1960. Photo dated: September 30, 1960. (Complements, LAPL).

**MATCHBOOKS.** Westchester Skateland, an indoor skating rink operated at Manchester and Florence Boulevards for many years, while Paradise Bowl on Sepulveda Boulevard was the areas first bowling alley. (Complements, Authors collection).

**Fritz Burns, 1953.** Aerial subdivider Fritz Burns, flying over a new Westchester housing development, dictating memos while inspecting the houses. (Complements, Life Magazine).

# LOS ANGELES TIMES-*HE TURNED DREAMS INTO REALITY*

December 16, 2001|CECILIA RASMUSSEN, TIMES STAFF WRITER

The legendary sleigh-pullers and jolly old St. Nick get better billing in the magic of Christmastime, but it was a maverick developer who became the king of low-cost housing who sparked a beloved holiday ritual for thousands of Angeleno families.

Fritz Burns was no Santa; he was thinking of ways to make money when, in 1953, he began a local yuletide tradition that enchanted children for decades: visiting Santa's live reindeer.

In late 1953, looking for a way to hype his sparkling new Panorama City shopping center in the San Fernando Valley, Burns added a mountain of fake snow, thousands of blinking lights and free candy canes, 96 giant white fir trees, Santa and six or seven (but not eight) tiny, white fallow deer, a small breed of reindeer, one of them wearing a fake red nose for Rudolph.
As Burns' reindeer multiplied with the same fervor with which they pulled Santa's sleigh, he began sending his growing flock of prancing little deer out to shopping centers throughout Los Angeles, not forgetting to put some on top of his one-story office building at the busy corner of Wilshire Boulevard and Highland Avenue.

The Christmas-reindeer stunt was the icing on the cake of a boom-and-bust career that took Burns from a seaside mansion to a tent, and back to prosperity again.

No developer saw the housing boom coming more clearly than Burns. He was a developer of near-mythic talent, a combination of optimism, patriotism and hype. In 1921, he arrived in Los Angeles to head the Minneapolis-based real estate firm of Dickinson & Gillespie. Immediately, he recognized Los Angeles as a developer's promised land and quickly began buying up acreage.

Luring crowds with a promise of a free ride in the company's biplane, at a time when flying in a plane was as exotic as riding a camel, Burns and his team of a hundred salesmen sold out 36 subdivisions within three years. His developments--from the San Gabriel Valley to the Westside--bore names like Hollydale Gardens, Alta Manor, Orange Blossom Manor, Poppyfields, Highway Highlands and Hollywood Laurelgrove.

In 1924, as wildcat oil wells began to spring up in Playa del Rey, Burns bought a large expanse of bluffs he called Palisades Del Rey, and there he built his own Italianate mansion on Waterview Street. CONT.

To entice buyers, he donated land for a university--now Loyola Marymount--persuaded city officials to build a municipal airport that eventually became Los Angeles International, and, at the base of the bluff, built the Del Rey Beach Club.

His company also set up picnic grounds in a shaded eucalyptus grove and sponsored a treasure hunt on the beach for prospective buyers. Big lots with underground utilities such as sewer lines sold for $200 to $500.

By the 1960s, jet-engine noise from LAX would render about 900 of the clifftop dwellings--within three subdivisions--unlivable. The homes were torn down in the 1970s, leaving behind ghostly vacant streets and foundations.
Burns was not only a believer in the promised land of Los Angeles, he also embraced some of its health crazes. Each morning, his crew of salesmen huffed and puffed as Burns put them through a challenging series of mandatory calisthenics.

In 1929, Burns bought out the company he had once worked for. A few weeks later, the stock market crashed and the 30-year-old self-made millionaire was almost instantly broke. His wife divorced him and he lived for the next five years in a tent on what was then known as Moonstone Beach--now Dockweiler State Beach--because of the stones that beachcombers found there. From there, he could look up and see his former mansion, and from there, too, he fought off creditors and wrote poems about his loneliness.

Despite his losses during the Depression, he hung onto most of his property. After the 1932 Olympics here, Burns scraped together enough money to buy, at $140 each, the prefabricated houses built to house the athletes. Mules dragged the two-room, rickety shacks from Baldwin Hills to Playa del Rey, where he rented them out as summer cottages along Trolley Way.

Burns began to recoup his fortune in earnest in 1934 when he hit oil at the corner of Manchester and Delgany avenues. With his hard-won wisdom, a new fortune and a new wife, he developed Windsor Hills, Westside Village and Toluca Woods, enterprises that marked his entry into home construction. From Maine to California, he recruited private builders under the umbrella of the group he formed in 1942, the National Assn. of Home Builders (NAHB).

Two years later, foreseeing that a fortune could be made when GIs came home from World War II to start families, he pushed a federal program that offered mortgages to veterans, and in 1945 teamed up with Henry J. Kaiser to form Kaiser Community Homes.

CONT.

New ideas about the American house were evolving, and technology was figuring into the evolution: how to produce houses using less material and labor. With this in mind, in 1946 Burns promoted the model "Home of Tomorrow," designed by architect Welton David Becket and located at Wilshire Boulevard and Highland Avenue. The postwar house featured many firsts, including an electric garbage disposal, intercoms, a touch-activated electrical system, "washable walls" and room-length closets.

A million visitors, handing over a buck a head, passed through the U-shaped house that Burns would soon use as his office. Starting in the Westchester area, he centered new housing projects on the aerospace industry, launching the "American Way of Life," which he billed as 1,000-plus square feet of hope for Depression-reared, war-weary GIs. The houses transformed the home-building business by using prefabricated parts and teams working in assembly-line fashion to cut costs. In 1948, he turned 800 acres of dairy barns and alfalfa fields into a community of identical homes on winding streets, each for $10,000 to $15,000, not far from where General Motors was building its biggest West Coast plant. It was named Panorama City.

Promoting the suburb, Burns persuaded his friend Art Linkletter to put Burns' radio stunt on his national radio show: Solve a riddle and win the grand prize, a fully furnished house with a car in the garage--and a job at Lockheed's nearby plant. Linkletter told listeners: "It's not just a house, it's a future."

Every week for 30 weeks, Linkletter read the riddle-poem and gave the only clue: **the answer was a place name.**

"Big Chief Windbag, gloomy and gay,
"I'm one over others that lie in decay.
"Where may I be found?
"Upon low ground . . .
"That's all, that's all I will say."

Listeners were held in thrall until Vivienne George, a 31-year-old office worker from Oregon, guessed the maddening riddle. The last line tipped her off. As a college journalism major, she learned to end her stories with "30," a notation to signify the end.

"That's all, that's all," she reasoned, could mean 30 degrees longitude and latitude, which pinpointed the location in Cairo, Egypt, a city at a low elevation built on ruins--decay. As for "Windbag," Cairo contains the letters "a-i-r."

CONT.

That same year, 1948, Burns and his wife, Gladys, bought silent-movie pioneering director David Wark Griffith's 300-acre ranch in Sylmar. Griffith Ranch, which Burns used as a weekend retreat, had been a location for early Western thrillers, such as "Custer's Last Stand" and Griffith's epic "Birth of a Nation." Burns perpetuated the Griffith name and soon opened the ranch gates to a herd bred from his own fallow deer.

By 1964, when his wife was named a delegate to the Republican National Convention in San Francisco, the reindeer had multiplied to 400. The couple organized a rally and picnic at the ranch for Barry Goldwater's campaign for president, offering supporters the chance to "put in a good word for Christmas with Rudolph." (Goldwater lost in a landslide.)

When the 1971 Sylmar earthquake collapsed a wall at the ranch, many reindeer escaped. The animals were becoming increasingly burdensome, and Burns advertised throughout the nation for charities and zoos to take them off his hands. Philippines President Ferdinand Marcos took some, and Mayor Tom Bradley presented some to the mayor of Nagoya, Japan.

The man who virtually built Subdivision Southern California--nearly 40,000 homes--died in 1979, leaving behind a large charitable foundation that still operates.

"Those who did not recognize him by his accomplishments," said Burns biographer James Thomas Keane, in his book "Fritz B. Burns and the Development of Los Angeles," "remembered him for the reindeer prancing atop his office and at shopping centers every Christmas."

**BACK FROM THE HURRICANE MARILYN, 1954**. Joe DiMaggio and Marilyn Monroe, returning to LAX at Westchester, CA, from the set of the "Seven Year Itch." Earlier that week, Monroe had posed for photographers while standing on a New York City subway grating, her white dress a-flutter around her hips. DiMaggio witnessed the scene and became furious. Shortly after this photo was taken, Monroe filed for divorce. She had come a long way from her days at Hawthorne, CA. (Courtesy, LAPL).

**NEW LIBRARY.** View of the facade of the Westchester Branch of the Los Angeles Public Library, 8956 Sepulveda Eastway, which opened July 13, 1952. (Courtesy, LAPL).

**TUG-OF-WAR, 1951**. Loyola freshman and sophomore class engage in a mud hole tug-of-war. (Courtesy, LAPL).

**BOB BOYD, 1950 LOYOLA UNIVERSITY CHAMPION.** Former Loyola football and track great, captured the 1950 NCAA men's track championship in the 100-yard dash with a time of 9.8 seconds. He later played seven seasons as a tight end for the National Football League's Los Angeles Rams, and led them to the 1951 World title. His most spectacular season was in 1954, when he caught 53 passes for 1,212 yards and 6 touchdowns. Boyd, who was elected to LMU's Hall of Fame in 1986, was one of the most versatile athletes in school history. In track, he established two all-time school records in the 100 yard dash (9.6 seconds) and the 220 yard dash (21.5 seconds) in 1950. (Courtesy, Loyola Marymount).

**WESTCHESTER STATION 5, LOS ANGELES FIRE DEPARTMENT.** Built at a cost of $109,000 ($107,700 for the structure and a mere $1,300 for the land), Old Fire Station 5 on Manchester Boulevard opened on August 2, 1950 to serve a City just beginning to realize the limits of its westward expansion to the nearby Pacific Coast. Over the years, Old Fire Station 5's physical space as well as electrical, mechanical, and plumbing systems was proving to be unable to support a modern and diverse workforce. Those working inside the nearly six-decade-old building experienced a daily struggle to effectively respond to the growing needs of the many now living, working and traveling in the Station's airport-adjacent district. (Complements, LAFD).

**FRITZ BURNS**. Looking over the sketches of the tremendous Hawaiian Village project are, from left to right: Fritz B. Burns; Mrs. Fritz B. Burns; Mrs. Henry J. Kaiser; F. Patrick Burns, manager of the project, and Industrialist Henry J. Kaiser. Photo dated: September 20, 1955. Along with being a prolific builder, Burns would for a time be President of Hilton Hotels, and along with his colleagues, invented the first "timeshare hotel." (Courtesy, LAPL). Below, Burns and Kaiser, 1956. (Courtesy, Life Magazine).

**HUGHES AIRCRAFT, 1952.** Aerial View of Hughes Aircraft and later Hughes Helicopters. Home of the HK-1 (aka ,The Spruce Goose), OH-6 Helicopter and the AH-64 Apache Helicopter . Note the farms north of Jefferson Boulevard. (Complements, David Coffin).

**NEW FIRE TRUCK FOR WESTCHESTER STATION 5, 1958.** Deputy Chief W.R. Goss and Fire Chief W.L. Miller present keys of new truck to Battalion Chief W.E. Olsen. (Courtesy, LAPL).

**NEW TUNNEL.** Westchester end of Hyperion tunnel, 15 January 1957. Shield holds back sand while muckers move sand to mucking machines. (Courtesy, LAPL).

**LOS ANGELES PACIFIC TROLLEY CARS, 1959; AWAITING DEMOLITION.** Prior to the advent of the automobile, the Westside of Los Angeles was opened to everyone by the Red Cars that serviced the region. From the Red Car stations at the Village of Playa del Rey, and at Culver and Jefferson Boulevards, it was a horse and buggy ride up the Bluffs to Westchester. Many of these street cars were submerged off Hermosa Beach Pier, to create an artificial reef, and remain there until this day. (Courtesy, Los Angeles Public Library).

**WESTCHESTER NEIGHBORLY LOVE.** Mrs. Viola E. Williams (left) and Mrs. Mae Baker stand at the fenced off sidewalk that separates their Westchester properties. "If one can't use it, no one can". June 18, 1951. (Courtesy, Whittier Library).

**VON'S MARKET, LA Tijera.** The vintage Von's Market, one of two in Westchester, originally had a huge "**V**" at the top of the sign. Charles Von der Ahe opened a cash and carry store named Von's Groceteria in downtown Los Angeles, California, in 1906. While I was writing this book, I learned that this store; one of the last great vintage markets in Westchester closed on July 14th, 2010. In 1948, Von's opened a pioneering store which offered self-service (i.e., pre-packaged) produce, meat, and deli items. By 1958, it had doubled in size to 27 stores, the third-largest grocery chain in the Greater Los Angeles Area. The Charles Von der Ahe Library (below, 1959), was the main library of Loyola Marymount University (LMU) until the Fall of 2009 when the new William H. Hannon Library was opened. In the new library there is a Von der Ahe suite located on the third floor. The original library construction was made possible by a 1957 gift from the Von's Foundation. Wil Von der Ahe was an alumnus of LMU's predecessor, Loyola University Los Angeles. (Complements, Author).

**LAX TAKE-OFF VIEW; SURFRIDGE, PLAYA DEL REY, 1939.** Many of the homes were custom built beach homes and cottages, owned by movie stars and luminaries of the time, including MGM Pictures mogul and Academy Award nominated director Cecil B. DeMille. The streets were originally part of a 1921 Dickinson & Gillespie Co. development called "Palisades Del Rey", billed as "The Last of the Beaches". Once an idyllic beachside community, comprised of over 800 homes on 470 acres, all that is left are the abandoned roads and a few walls and fences. Streets like: Ivalee, Jacqueline, Napoleon, Waterview, Rindge and Kilgore are there, but the homes are gone, having fallen prey in the late 60's and early 70's to four forced rounds of condemnations by the City of Los Angeles and LAX. (Courtesy, Los Angeles Public Library).

**PEREIRA HALL.** Photograph of an exterior view of Pereira Hall, the newly completed Engineering Building at Loyola University, 1955. (Courtesy, LAPL).

**CANTINFLAS.** Arriving at LAX in Westchester, 4 July 1958. Cantinflas was an actor and Mexican entertainer. Charlie Chaplin once called him "the greatest comedian in the world." (Complements, LAPL).

**DISNEYLAND; LOS ANGELES AIRWAYS, 1956.** Los Angeles Airways Sikorsky S-55 (N736A) landing at the Disneyland Heliport in 1956. From 1955 to 1968, Los Angeles Airways provided regularly scheduled helicopter passenger service between Disneyland and Los Angeles International Airport and other cities in the area. The helicopters initially operated from Disneyland Heliport, located behind Tomorrowland. Service later moved, in 1960, to a new heliport north of the Disneyland Hotel. Arriving guests were transported to the Disneyland Hotel via tram. (Complements, LAPL).

**PARADISE THEATRE,1950.** The Paradise Theatre in Westchester was located a few blocks south of the Fox Loyola Theater. It opened in 1950. The front is of field-stone, brick and glass in the modern California style. Live plants under the canopy gave this area an outdoor patio effect. After passing through a mirrored and planted lobby with a curved refreshment stand and a manager's office at one side, the patron entered a magnificent foyer with pastel walls trimmed in redwood and aquamarine carpeting studded with yellow and beige stars. The last chain to operate the Paradise Theater was Pacific Theaters, and it later ran as an independent for a short time before being gutted and turned into an office building. Buried in the sidewalks under engraved brass plaques, movie memorabilia from bygone days sit there still. (Complements, Cinema Treasures).

**HELEN KELLER, ARRVING AT LAX, 1955.** (Complements, LAPL).

**1958, LAX.** View of a BOAC Bristol Britannia Turbo-Prop transport, at LAX. (Complements, LAPL).

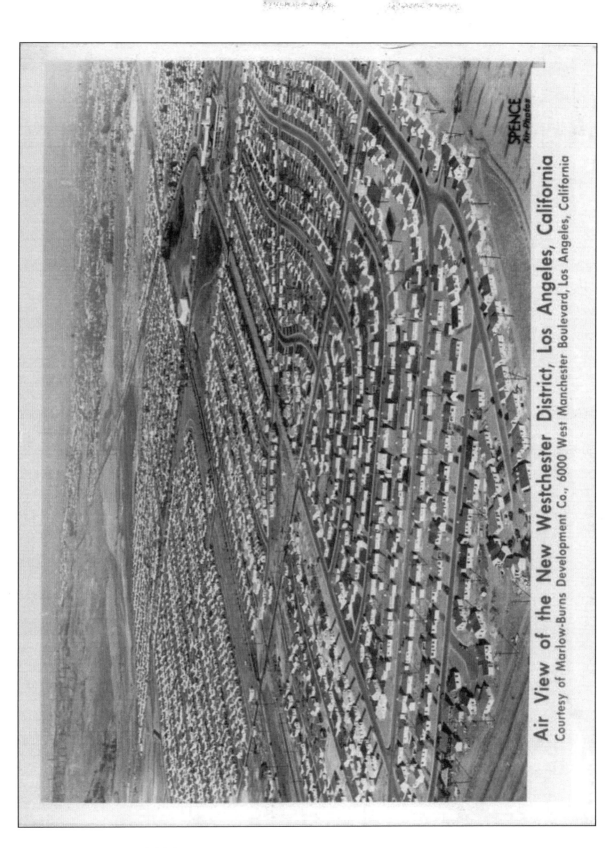

Air View of the New Westchester District, Los Angeles, California
Courtesy of Marlow-Burns Development Co., 6000 West Manchester Boulevard, Los Angeles, California

SPENCE
Air Photos

**1948**. (Courtesy, LAPL).

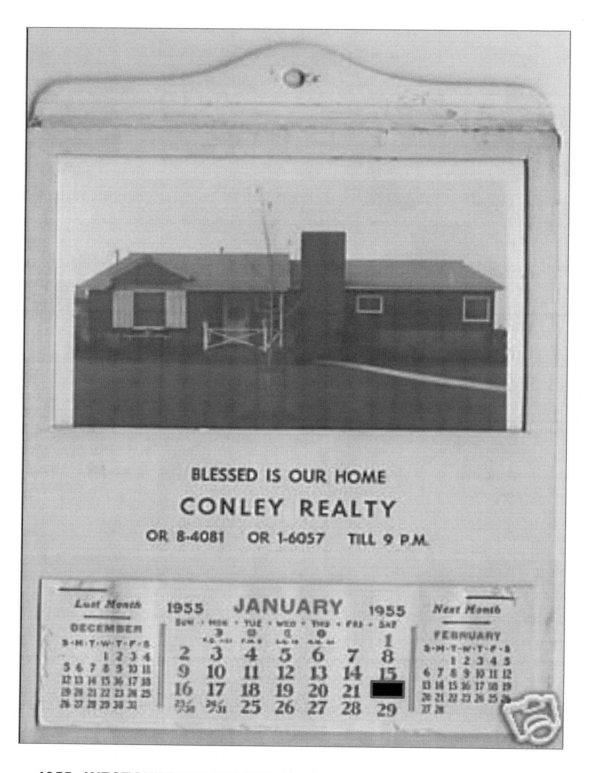

**1955, WESTCHESTER CALENDAR.** This is a view of a home on Henefer Avenue, in Westchester. (Complements, Author).

**DANIEL FREEMAN HOME, 1972.** *The Centinela*; just before demolition, at 333 Prairie Avenue. Daniel Freeman named the street because the area reminded him of the vast empty prairie's of his native Canada. (Complements, Author).

**POSTCARDS, 1960, LOYOLA UNIVERSITY**. Inset, Loyola Dorm. Rooms.
(Courtesy, Authors Collection).

**MARILYN MONROE, 1959, LAX.** Actress Marilyn Monroe is accompanied by her husband, playwright Arthur Miller, as she arrives at Los Angeles International Airport from New York to start work on a 20th Century-Fox picture *(Let's Make Love*, 1960). (Courtesy, Los Angeles Times; Publication date: November 4, 1959).

**WESTCHESTER CHRISTMAS CANDLE, 1960.** Dick Birch paints a
finished  Christmas decorative 'candle' for outdoor displays.  He made a
sign;  "Birch," as well. (Complements, Google Books).